EP
12/22

£1.00

How to Mix Drinks

or

The Bon Vivant's Companion

How to Mix Drinks
or
The Bon Vivant's Companion

Jerry Thomas

With contemporary illustrations

ET REMOTISSIMA PROPE

Hesperus Classics
Published by Hesperus Press Limited
4 Rickett Street, London sw6 1ru
www.hesperuspress.com

First published in 1862
First published by Hesperus Press Limited, 2008

Designed and typeset by Fraser Muggeridge studio
Printed in Jordan by Jordan National Press

ISBN: 978-184391-187-6

CONTENTS

PREFACE TO THE FIRST EDITION

In all the ages of the world, and in all countries, men have indulged in 'social drinks'. They have always possessed themselves of some popular beverage apart from water and those of the breakfast and tea table. Whether it is judicious that mankind should continue to indulge in such things, or whether it would be wiser to abstain from all enjoyments of that character, it is not our province to decide. We leave that question to the moral philosopher. We simply contend that a relish for 'social drinks' is universal, that those drinks exist in greater variety in the United States than in any other country in the world; and that he, therefore, who proposes to impart to these drinks not only the most palatable but the most wholesome characteristics of which they may be made susceptible, is a genuine public benefactor. That is exactly our object in introducing this little volume to the public. We do not propose to persuade any man to drink, for instance, a julep, or a cocktail, who has never happened to make the acquaintance of those refreshing articles under circumstances calculated to induce more intimate relations; but we *do* propose to instruct those whose 'intimate relations' in question render them somewhat fastidious, in the daintiest fashions thereunto pertaining.

We very well remember seeing one day in London, in the rear of the Bank of England, a small drinking saloon that had been set up by a peripatetic American, at the door of which was placed a board covered with the unique titles of the American mixed drinks supposed to be prepared within that limited establishment. The 'Connecticut eye-openers' and 'Alabama fog-cutters', together with the 'lightning-smashes' and the 'thunderbolt-cocktails', created a profound sensation in the crowd assembled to peruse the Nectarine bill of fare, if they did not produce custom. It struck us, then, that a list of all the social drinks – the composite beverages, if we may call them so – of America, would really be one of the curiosities of jovial literature; and that if it was combined with a catalogue of the mixtures common to other nations, and made practically useful by the addition of a concise description of the various processes for 'brewing' each, it would be a 'blessing to mankind'. There would be no excuse for imbibing, with such a book at hand, the 'villainous compounds' of bar-keeping Goths and Vandals, who know no more of the amenities of *bon vivant* existence than a Hottentot can know of the *bouquet* of champagne.

'There's philosophy,' said Father Tom in the drama, 'even in a jug of punch.' We claim the credit of 'philosophy teaching by example', then, to no ordinary extent in the composition of this volume; for our index exhibits the title of eighty-six different kinds of punches, together with a universe of cobblers, juleps, bitters, cups, slings, shrubs, etc., each and all of which the reader is care-fully educated how to concoct in the choicest manner. For the perfection of this education, the name, alone, of *Jerry Thomas* is a sufficient guarantee. He has travelled Europe and America in search of all that is recondite in this branch of the spirit art. He has been the Jupiter Olympus of the bar at the Metropolitan Hotel in this city. He was the presiding deity at the Planters' House, St Louis. He has been the proprietor of one of the most recherché saloons in New Orleans as well as in New York. His very name is synonymous, in the lexicon of mixed drinks, with all that is rare and original. To *The Wine Press*, edited by F.S. Cozzens, Esq., we are indebted for the composition of several valuable punches, and among them we may particularize the celebrated 'Nuremburgh', and the equally famous 'Philadelphia Fish-House' punch. The rest we owe to the inspiration of Jerry Thomas himself, and as he is as inexorable as the Medes and Persians in his principle that no excellent drink can be made out of anything but excellent materials, we conceive that we are safe in asserting that whatever may be prepared after his instructions will be able to speak eloquently for itself. 'Good wine needs no bush,' Shakespeare tells us, and over one of Jerry's mixtures eulogy is quite as redundant.

How to Mix Drinks
or
The Bon Vivant's Companion

PUNCH

To make punch of any sort in perfection, the ambrosial essence of the lemon must be extracted by rubbing lumps of sugar on the rind, which breaks the delicate little vessels that contain the essence, and at the same time absorbs it. This, and making the mixture sweet and strong, using tea instead of water, and thoroughly amalgamating all the compounds, so that the taste of neither the bitter, the sweet, the spirit, nor the element, shall be perceptible one over the other, is the grand secret, only to be acquired by practice.

In making hot toddy, or hot punch, you must put in the spirits before the water: in cold punch, grog, etc., the other way.

The precise proportions of spirit and water, or even of the acidity and sweetness, can have no general rule, as scarcely two persons make punch alike.

I

BRANDY PUNCH

Use large bar glass

One teaspoon of raspberry syrup
Two tablespoons of white sugar
One wineglass of water
One and one-half wineglasses
    of brandy

One-half small-sized lemon
Two slices of orange
One piece of pineapple

Fill the tumbler with shaved ice, shake well, and dress the top with berries in season. Sip through a straw.

BRANDY PUNCH

For a party of twenty

One gallon of water
Three quarts of brandy
One-half pint of Jamaica rum
Two pounds of sugar
Juice of six lemons
Ice, and add berries in season

Three oranges sliced
One pineapple, pared,
   and cut up
One gill of curaçao
Two gills of raspberry syrup

Mix the materials well together in a large bowl, and you have a splendid punch.

MISSISSIPPI PUNCH

Use large bar glass

One wineglass of brandy
One-half wineglass of
   Jamaica rum
One-half wineglass of
   Bourbon whiskey

One and one-half tablespoons
   of powdered white sugar
One-quarter of a large lemon
One-half wineglass of water
Fill a tumbler with shaved ice

The above must be well shaken, and to those who like their draughts 'like linked sweetness long drawn out', let them use a glass tube or straw to sip the nectar through. The top of this punch should be ornamented with small pieces of orange, and berries in season.

HOT BRANDY AND RUM PUNCH

For a party of fifteen

One quart of Jamaica rum
One quart of Cognac brandy
One pound of white loaf sugar

Four lemons
Three quarts of boiling water
One teaspoon of nutmeg

Rub the sugar over the lemons until it has absorbed all the yellow part of the skins, then put the sugar into a punchbowl; add the ingredients well together, pour over them the boiling water, stir well together; add the rum, brandy and nutmeg; mix thoroughly, and the punch will be ready to serve. As we have before said, it is very important, in making good punch, that all the ingredients are thoroughly incorporated; and, to ensure success, the process of mixing must be diligently attended to. Allow a quart for four persons; but this information must be taken *cum grano salis*;[1] for the capacities of persons for this kind of beverage are generally supposed to vary considerably.

SCOTCH WHISKY PUNCH

Steep the thin yellow shavings of lemon peel in the whisky, which should be of the best quality; the sugar should be dissolved in boiling water. As it requires *genius* to make whisky punch, it would be impertinent to give proportions.

WHISKEY PUNCH

One wineglass of whiskey
   (Irish or Scotch)
Sugar to taste

Two wineglasses of boiling
   water

Dissolve the sugar well with one wineglass of the water, then pour in the whiskey, and add the balance of the water. Sweeten to taste, and put in a small piece of lemon rind, or a thin slice of lemon.

COLD WHISKEY PUNCH

Use large bar glass

One tablespoon of powdered
   white sugar dissolved in
   a little water
Juice of half a small lemon

One and one-half
   wineglasses of Irish
   or Scotch whiskey

Fill the glass with shaved ice, shake well, and dress the top with two thin slices of lemon, and berries in season. Serve with a straw.

This beverage ought always to be made with boiling water, and allowed to concoct and cool for a day or two before it is put on the table. In this way, the materials get more intensely amalgamated than *cold* water and *cold* whiskey ever get. As to the beautiful mutual adaptation of cold rum and cold water, that is beyond all praise, being one of nature's most exquisite achievements.

IRISH WHISKEY PUNCH

This is the genuine Irish beverage. It is generally made one-third pure whiskey, and two-thirds boiling water, in which the sugar has been dissolved. If lemon punch, the rind is rubbed on the sugar, and a small proportion of juice added before the whiskey is poured in.

Irish whiskey is not fit to drink until it is three years old.

GIN PUNCH

Use large bar glass

One tablespoon of raspberry syrup

Two tablespoons of white sugar

One and one-half wineglasses of gin

One-half of a small-sized lemon

Two slices of orange

One piece of pineapple

One wineglass of water

Fill the tumbler with shaved ice. Shake well, and ornament the top with berries in season. Sip through a glass tube or straw.

10

GIN PUNCH

From a recipe by Soyer[2]

One-half pint of old gin
One gill of maraschino
The juice of two lemons
The rind of half a lemon

Four ounces of syrup
One quart bottle of German
   seltzer water
Ice well

11

CHAMPAGNE PUNCH

One quart bottle of wine
One quarter pound of sugar
One orange, sliced
The juice of a lemon
Three slices of pineapple

One wineglass of raspberry
   or strawberry syrup
Ornament with fruits in season,
   and serve in champagne
   goblets

This can be made in any quantity by observing the proportions of the ingredients as given above. Four bottles of wine make a gallon, and a gallon is generally sufficient for fifteen persons in a mixed party. For a good champagne punch, see Rocky Mountain Punch, No. 43.

SHERRY PUNCH

Use large bar glass

Two wineglasses of sherry
One tablespoon of sugar

Two or three slices of orange
Two or three slices of lemon

Fill tumbler with shaved ice, shake well, and ornament with berries in season. Sip through a straw.

CLARET PUNCH

Use large bar glass

One and one-half tablespoons
  of sugar

Two or three slices of orange
One slice of lemon

Fill the tumbler with shaved ice, and then pour in your claret, shake well, and ornament with berries in season. Place a straw in the glass. To make a quantity of claret punch, see Imperial Punch, No. 41.

SAUTERNE PUNCH

Use large bar glass

The same as claret punch, using sauterne instead of claret.

PORT WINE PUNCH

Use large bar glass

The same as claret punch, using port wine instead of claret, and ornament with berries in season.

VANILLA PUNCH

Use large bar glass

One tablespoon of sugar	The juice of one-quarter of
One wineglass of brandy	a lemon

Fill the tumbler with shaved ice, shake well, ornament with one or two slices of lemon, and flavor with a few drops of vanilla extract.

This is a delicious drink, and should be imbibed through a glass tube or straw.

PINEAPPLE PUNCH

For a party of ten

Four bottles of champagne
One pint of Jamaica rum
One pint of brandy
One gill of curaçao

Juice of four lemons
Four pineapples sliced
Sweeten to taste with
  pulverized white sugar

Put the pineapple with one pound of sugar in a glass bowl, and let them stand until the sugar is well soaked in the pineapple, then add all the other ingredients, except the champagne. Let this mixture stand in ice for about an hour, then add the champagne. Place a large block of ice in the center of the bowl, and ornament it with loaf sugar, sliced orange, and other fruits in season.

Serve in champagne glasses.

Pineapple punch is sometimes made by adding sliced pineapple to brandy punch.

ORGEAT PUNCH

Use large bar glass

One and one-half tablespoons
  of orgeat syrup
One and one-half wineglasses
  of brandy

Juice of one-half a lemon,
  and fill the tumbler with
  shaved ice

Shake well, ornament with berries in season, and dash port wine on top.

Place the straw as in a mint julep.

CURAÇAO PUNCH

Use large bar glass

One tablespoon of sugar
One wineglass of brandy
One-half wineglass of Jamaica
   rum

One wineglass of water
One-half pony glass of curaçao
The juice of half a lemon

Fill the tumbler with shaved ice, shake well, and ornament with fruits of the season. Sip the nectar through a straw.

ROMAN PUNCH

Use large bar glass

One tablespoon of sugar
One tablespoon of raspberry
   syrup
One teaspoon of curaçao

One wineglass of Jamaica rum
One-half wineglass of brandy
The juice of half a lemon

Fill with shaved ice, shake well, dash with port wine, and ornament with fruits in season. Imbibe through a straw.

MILK PUNCH

Use large bar glass

One tablespoon of fine white sugar

Two tablespoons of water

One wineglass of Cognac brandy

One-half wineglass of Santa Cruz rum

One-third tumblerful of shaved ice

Fill with milk, shake the ingredients well together, and grate a little nutmeg on top.

HOT MILK PUNCH

Use large bar glass

This punch is made the same as No. 21, with the exception that hot milk is used, and no ice.

MANHATTAN MILK PUNCH

Same as the following *cold* milk punch, with the addition of five drops of aromatic tincture.

EGG MILK PUNCH

Use large bar glass

One teaspoon of fine white sugar
One wineglass of brandy
One-fourth wineglass of Santa
    Cruz rum

One egg
Small lump of ice

Fill the glass with pure fresh milk, shake the ingredients well together, and strain into a large glass.

ENGLISH MILK PUNCH

Put the following ingredients into a very clean pitcher, viz.:

The juice of six lemons
The rind of two lemons
One pound of sugar
One pineapple, peeled, sliced
    and pounded
One gill of arrack*
One quart of boiling water

One small stick of cinnamon
One pint of brandy
One pint of rum
Twenty coriander seeds
Six cloves
One cup of strong green tea

The boiling water to be added last; cork this down to prevent evaporation, and allow these ingredients to steep for at least six hours; then add a quart of hot milk and the juice of two lemons; mix, and filter through a jelly-bag; and when the punch has passed bright, put it away in tight-corked bottles. This punch is intended to be iced for drinking.

* Most of the arrack imported into this country is distilled from rice, and comes from Batavia. It is little used in America, except to flavor punch; the taste of it is very agreeable in this mixture. Arrack improves much with age. It is much used in some parts of India, where it is distilled from *toddy*, the juice of the coconut tree. An imitation of arrack is made by adding to a bowl of punch a few grains of benzoin, or Flowers of Benjamin.

ENGLISH MILK PUNCH

Another method

This seductive and nectareous drink can also be made by the directions herewith given:

To two quarts of water add one quart of milk. Mix one quart of old Jamaica rum with two of French brandy, and put the spirit to the milk, stirring it for a short time; let it stand for an hour, but do not suffer anyone of delicate appetite to see the melange in its present state as the sight might create a distaste for the punch when perfected. Filter through blotting paper into bottles; and should you find that the liquid is cloudy, when it should not be, you may clarify it by adding a small portion of isinglass to each bottle. The above recipe will furnish you with half a dozen of punch.

PUNCH À LA FORD

A recipe from Benson E. Hill, Esq., author of *The Epicure's Almanac*

'The late General Ford, who for many years was the commanding engineer at Dover, kept a most hospitable board, and used to make punch on a large scale, after the following method:

'He would select three dozen of lemons, the coats of which were smooth, and whose rinds were not too thin; these he would peel with a sharp knife into a large earthen vessel, taking care that none of the rind should be detached but that portion in which the cells are placed, containing the essential oil; when he had completed the first part of the process, he added two pounds of lump sugar, and stirred the peel and sugar together with an oar-shaped piece of wood, for nearly half an hour, thereby extracting a greater quantity of the essential oil. Boiling water was next poured into the vessel, and the whole well stirred, until the sugar was completely dissolved. The lemons were then cut and squeezed, the juice strained from the kernels; these were placed in a separate jug, and boiling water poured upon them, the general being aware that the pips were enveloped in a thick mucilage, full of flavor; half the lemon juice was now thrown in; and as soon as the kernels were free from their transparent coating, their liquor was strained and added.

'The sherbet was now tasted, more acid or more sugar applied as required, and care taken not to render the lemonade too watery. "Rich of the fruit, and plenty of sweetness," was the General's maxim. The sherbet was then measured, and to every three quarts a pint of Cognac brandy and a pint of old Jamaica rum were allotted, the spirit being well stirred as poured in; bottling immediately followed, and, when completed, the beverage was kept in a cold cellar, or tank, till required. At the General's table I have frequently drunk punch thus made, more than six months old; and found it much improved by time and a cool atmosphere.'

PUNCH JELLY

Make a good bowl of punch, à la Ford, already described. To every pint of punch add an ounce and a half of isinglass, dissolved in a quarter of a pint of water (about half a tumbler full); pour this into the punch whilst quite hot, and then fill your molds, taking care that they are not disturbed until the jelly is completely set.

Orange, lemon, or calf's-foot jelly, not used at dinner, can be converted into punch jelly for the evening, by following the above directions, only taking care to omit a portion of the acid prescribed in making the sherbet.

This preparation is a very agreeable refreshment on a cold night, but should be used in moderation; the strength of the punch is so artfully concealed by its admixture with the gelatine, that many persons, particularly of the softer sex, have been tempted to partake so plentifully of it as to render them somewhat unfit for waltzing or quadrilling after supper.

GLASGOW PUNCH

From a recipe in the possession of Dr Shelton Mackenzie

Melt lump sugar in cold water, with the juice of a couple of lemons, passed through a fine hair-strainer. This is sherbet, and must be well mingled. Then add old Jamaica rum – one part of rum to five of sherbet. Cut a couple of limes in two, and run each section rapidly around the edge of the jug or bowl, gently squeezing in some of the delicate acid. This done, the punch is made. Imbibe.

REGENT'S PUNCH

For a party of twenty

Three bottles of champagne
One bottle of Hockheimer
One bottle of curaçao
One bottle of Cognac
Four pounds of bloom raisins

One half-bottle of Jamaica rum
Two bottles of Madeira
Two bottles of seltzer, or plain
   soda water

To which add oranges, lemons, rock candy, and instead of water, green tea to taste. Refrigerate with all the icy power of the Arctic.

REGENT'S PUNCH

Another recipe
From *The Bordeaux Wine and Liquor Guide*

One and one-half pint each of
   strong hot green tea, lemon
   juice, and capillaire

One bottle of champagne
One pint each of rum, brandy,
   arrack, and curaçao

Mix, and place a slice of pineapple into it.

RASPBERRY PUNCH

From *The Bordeaux Wine and Liquor Guide*

One and one-half gill of
  raspberry juice, or vinegar
Three and one-half pints of
  boiling water

Three-quarters of a pound
  of lump sugar

Infuse half an hour, strain, add one-half pint of porter, three-quarters to one pint, each, of rum and brandy (or either one and one-half to two pints), and add more water and sugar, if desired weaker or sweeter. A liqueur glass of curaçao, noyau, or maraschino improves it.

NATIONAL GUARD
7TH REGIMENT PUNCH

Use large bar glass

One tablespoon of sugar
The juice of a quarter of a lemon
One wineglass of brandy

One wineglass of Catawba
  wine
Flavor with raspberry syrup

Fill the glass with shaved ice. Shake and mix thoroughly, then ornament with slices of orange, pineapple, and berries in season, and dash with Jamaica rum. This delicious beverage should be imbibed through a straw.

34

ST CHARLES' PUNCH

Use large bar glass

One tablespoon of sugar
One wineglass of port wine
One pony of brandy

The juice of one-fourth
of a lemon

Fill the tumbler with shaved ice, shake well, ornament with fruits in season, and serve with a straw.

35

69TH REGIMENT PUNCH

In earthen mug

One-half wineglass of Irish
whiskey
One-half wineglass of Scotch
whisky

One piece of lemon
One teaspoon of sugar
Two wineglasses of hot water

This is a capital punch for a cold night.

36

LOUISIANA SUGAR
HOUSE PUNCH

From a recipe in the possession of Colonel T.B. Thorpe[3]

To one quart of boiling syrup, taken from the kettles, add whiskey or brandy to suit the *patient*. Flavor with the juice of sour oranges.

37

DRY PUNCH

From a recipe by *Santina*, the celebrated Spanish caterer

Two gallons of brandy
One gallon of water
One-half gallon of tea
One pint of Jamaica rum

One-half pint of curaçao
Juice of six lemons
One and one-half pounds
   of white sugar

Mix thoroughly, and strain, as already described in the recipe for Punch à la Ford, adding more sugar and lemon juice, to taste. Bottle, and keep on ice for three or four days, and the punch will be ready for use; but the longer it stands, the better it gets.

38

LA PATRIA PUNCH

For a party of twenty

Three bottles of champagne,
  iced
One bottle of Cognac

Six oranges
One pineapple

Slice the oranges and pineapple in a bowl, pour the Cognac over them, and let them steep for a couple of hours, then in with the champagne and serve immediately.

39

SPREAD EAGLE PUNCH

One bottle of Scotch whisky
One bottle of rye whiskey

Lemon peel, sugar, and
  boiling water at discretion

ROCHESTER PUNCH

For a party of twenty
From a recipe in the possession of Roswell Hart, Esq.[4]

Two bottles of sparkling Catawba
Two bottles of sparkling Isabella
One bottle of sauterne

Two wineglasses of
  maraschino
Two wineglasses of curaçao

Fill the tranquil bowl with ripe strawberries. Should the strawberry season be over, or under, add a few drops of extract of peach or vanilla.

IMPERIAL PUNCH

One bottle of claret
One bottle of soda water
Four tablespoons of powdered
  white sugar
One-quarter teaspoon of grated
  nutmeg

One liqueur glass of
  maraschino
About one-half pound of ice
Three or four slices of
  cucumber rind

Put all the ingredients into a bowl or pitcher and mix well.

THIRTY-SECOND REGIMENT
OR VICTORIA PUNCH

For a party of twenty
Recipe from the late Wm. H. Herbert, Esq.[5]

Six lemons, in slices
One-half gallon of brandy
One-half gallon of Jamaica rum
One pound of white sugar

One and three-quarters quarts
of water
One pint of boiling milk

Steep the lemons for twenty-four hours in the brandy and rum; add the sugar, water, and milk and, when well mixed, strain through a jelly-bag.

This punch may be bottled, and used afterward hot or cold.

Half the above quantity, or even less, may be made, as this recipe is for a party of twenty.

ROCKY MOUNTAIN PUNCH

For a mixed party of twenty
From a recipe in the possession of Major James Foster
This delicious punch is composed as follows:

Five bottles of champagne   Six lemons, sliced
One quart of Jamaica rum   Sugar to taste
One pint of maraschino

Mix the above ingredients in a large punch bowl, then place in the center of the bowl a large square block of ice, ornamented with rock candy, loaf sugar, sliced lemons or oranges, and fruits in season. This is a splendid punch for New Year's Day.

44

PUNCH GRASSOT

The following recipe was given by M. Grassot,
the eminent French comedian of the Palais Royal,
to Mr Howard Paul, the celebrated entertainer,
when performing in Paris.

One wineglass of brandy   One quarter of a pint of water
Five drops of curaçao   The peel of a small lemon,
One drop of acetic acid   sliced
Two teaspoons of simple syrup

Mix, serve up with ice, in large goblet, and if possible, garnish the top with a slice of peach or apricot. In cold weather this punch is admirable served hot.

45

LIGHT GUARD PUNCH*

For a party of twenty

Three bottles of champagne
One bottle of pale sherry
One bottle of Cognac

One bottle of sauterne
One pineapple, sliced
Four lemons, sliced

Sweeten to taste, mix in a punch bowl, cool with a large lump of ice, and serve immediately.

* This is sufficient for a mixed party of twenty, not twenty of the Light Guard.

46

PHILADELPHIA FISH-HOUSE PUNCH

From a recipe in the possession of Charles G. Leland, Esq.[6]

One pint of mixture, composed
of one-fourth pint of peach
brandy, one-half pint
of Cognac brandy, and one-
fourth pint of Jamaica rum

One-third pint of lemon juice
Three-quarters pound of
white sugar
Two and one-half pints
of cold water

The above is generally sufficient for one person.

NON-SUCH PUNCH

Six bottles of claret
Six bottles of soda water
One bottle of brandy
One bottle of sherry

One-half pint of green tea
Juice of three lemons
One-half of a pineapple cut up
   in small pieces

Sweeten with white sugar to taste. Strain a bottle immediately. Keep for one month before using. This is a delicious and safe drink for a mixed evening party. Cool before serving.

CANADIAN PUNCH

Two quarts of rye whiskey
One pint of Jamaica rum
Six lemons, sliced

One pineapple, sliced
Four quarts of water

Sweeten to taste, and ice.

49

TIP TOP PUNCH

For a party of five

One bottle of champagne	Two tablespoons of powdered
Two bottles of soda water	sugar
One liqueur glass of curaçao	One slice of pineapple, cut up

Put all the ingredients together in a small bowl, mix well, ice and serve in champagne goblets.

50

ARRACK PUNCH

In making 'rack punch, you ought to put two glasses (wine glasses) of rum to three of arrack. A good deal of sugar is required; but sweetening, after all, must be left to taste. Lemons and limes are also matter of palate, but two lemons are enough for the above quantity; put then an equal quantity of water – i.e. not five but *six* to allow for the lemon juice, and you have a very pretty three tumblers of punch.

ARRACK PUNCH

Another recipe

Steep in one quart of old Batavia arrack, six lemons cut in thin slices, for six hours. At the end of that time, the lemon must be removed without squeezing. Dissolve one pound of loaf sugar in one quart of boiling water, and add the hot solution to the arrack. Let it stand to cool. This is a delightful liqueur, and should be used as such.

52

BIMBO PUNCH

Bimbo is made nearly in the same way as the above, except that Cognac brandy is substituted for arrack.

53

COLD PUNCH

Arrack, port wine and water, of each two pints, one pound of loaf sugar, and the juice of eight lemons.

NUREMBURGH PUNCH

For a party of fifteen
From a recipe in possession of Hon. Gulian C. Verplanck[7]

Take three-quarters of a pound of loaf sugar, press upon it, through muslin, the juice of two or more good-sized oranges; add a little of the peel, cut very thin, pour upon a quart of boiling water, the third part of that quantity of Batavia arrack, and a bottle of hot, but not boiling, red or white French wine – red is best. Stir together. This is excellent when cold, and will improve by age.

55

UNITED SERVICE PUNCH

Dissolve, in two pints of hot tea, three-quarters of a pound of loaf sugar, having previously rubbed off, with a portion of the sugar, the peel of four lemons; then add the juice of eight lemons, and a pint of arrack.

56

RUBY PUNCH

Dissolve, in three pints of hot tea, one pound of sugar; add thereto the juice of six lemons, a pint of arrack, and a pint of port wine.

ROYAL PUNCH

To be drunk as hot as possible

One pint of hot green tea
One-half pint of brandy
One-half pint of Jamaica rum
One wineglass of curaçao
One wineglass of arrack

Juice of two limes
A thin slice of lemon
White sugar to taste
One gill of warm
   calf's-foot jelly

This is a composition worthy of a king, and the materials are admirably blended; the inebriating effects of the spirits being deadened by the tea, whilst the jelly softens the mixture, and destroys the acrimony of the acid and sugar. The whites of a couple of eggs well beat up to a froth, may be substituted for the jelly where that is not at hand. If the punch is too strong, add more green tea to taste.

CENTURY CLUB PUNCH

Two parts old Santa Cruz rum; one part old Jamaica rum, five parts water; lemons and sugar *ad lib*. This is a nice punch.

59

DUKE OF NORFOLK PUNCH

In twenty quarts of French brandy put the peels of thirty lemons and thirty oranges, pared so thin that not the least of the white is left. Infuse twelve hours. Have ready thirty quarts of cold water that has boiled; put to it fifteen pounds of double-refined sugar; and when well mixed, pour it upon the brandy and peels, adding the juice of the oranges and of twenty-four lemons; mix well, then strain through a very fine hair-sieve, into a very clean barrel that has held high spirits, and put in two quarts of new milk. Stir, and then bung it close; let it stand six weeks in a warm cellar; bottle the liquor for use, observing great care that the bottles are perfectly clean and dry, and the corks of the best quality, and well put in. This liquor will keep many years, and improve by age.

60

DUKE OF NORFOLK PUNCH

Another recipe

Pare six lemons and three oranges very thin, squeeze the juice into a large teapot, put to it two quarts of brandy, one of white wine, and one of milk, and one pound and a quarter of sugar. Let it be mixed, and then covered for twenty-four hours, strain through a jelly-bag till clear, then bottle it.

61

QUEEN PUNCH

Put two ounces of cream of tartar, and the juice and parings of two lemons, into a stone jar; pour on them seven quarts of boiling water, stir and cover close. When cold, sweeten with loaf sugar, and straining it, bottle and cork it tight. This is a very pleasant liquor, and very wholesome; but from the latter consideration was at one time drunk in such quantities as to become injurious. Add, in bottling, half a pint of rum to the whole quantity.

62

GOTHIC PUNCH

For a party of ten
From a recipe in the possession of Bayard Taylor, Esq.[8]

Four bottles of still Catawba, one bottle of claret, three oranges, or one pineapple, ten tablespoons of sugar. Let this mixture stand in a very cold place, or in ice, for one hour or more, then add one bottle of champagne.

63

OXFORD PUNCH

We have been favored by an English gentleman with the following recipe for the concoction of punch as drunk by the students of the University of Oxford:

Rub the rinds of three fresh lemons with loaf sugar till you have extracted a portion of the juice; cut the peel finely off two lemons more, and two sweet oranges. Add six glasses of calf's-foot jelly; let all be put into a large jug, and stir well together. Pour in two quarts of water boiling hot, and set the jug upon the hob for twenty minutes. Strain the liquor through a fine sieve into a large bowl; put in a bottle of capillaire, half a pint of sherry, a pint of Cognac brandy, a pint of old Jamaica rum, and a quart of orange shrub; stir well as you pour in the spirit. If you find it requires some more sweetness, add sugar to your taste.

UNCLE TOBY PUNCH

English

Take two large fresh lemons with rough skins, quite ripe, and some large lumps of double-refined sugar. Rub the sugar over the lemons till it has absorbed all the yellow part of the skins. Then put into the bowl these lumps, and as much more as the juice of the lemons may be supposed to require; for no certain weight can be mentioned, as the acidity of a lemon cannot be known till tried, and therefore this must be determined by the taste. Then squeeze the lemon juice upon the sugar; and, with a bruiser press the sugar and the juice particularly well together, for a great deal of the richness and fine flavor of the punch depends on this rubbing and mixing process being thoroughly performed. Then mix this up very well with boiling water (soft water is best) till the whole is rather cool. When this mixture (which is now called the sherbet) is to your taste, take brandy and rum in equal quantities, and put them to it, mixing the whole well together again. The quantity of liquor must be according to your taste; two good lemons are generally enough to make four quarts of punch, including a quart of liquor, with half a pound of sugar; but this depends much on the taste, and on the strength of the spirit.

As the pulp is disagreeable to some persons, the sherbet may be strained before the liquor is put in. Some strain the lemon before they put it to the sugar, which is improper, as, when the pulp and sugar are well mixed together, it adds much to the richness of the punch.

When only rum is used, about half a pint of porter will soften the punch; and even when both rum and brandy are used, the porter gives a richness, and to some a very pleasant flavor.

CAPILLAIRE

Put a wineglass of curaçao into a pint of clarified syrup, shake them well together, and pour it into the proper sized bottles. A tea-spoon in a glass of fair water makes a pleasant *eau sacre*.

CAPILLAIRE

Another recipe

To one gallon of water add twenty-eight pounds of loaf sugar; put both over the fire to simmer; when milk-warm add the whites of four or five eggs, well beaten; as these simmer with the syrup, skim it well; then pour it off, and flavor it with orange flower water or bitter almonds, whichever you prefer.

PUNCH À LA ROMAINE

For a party of fifteen

Take the juice of ten lemons and two sweet oranges, dissolve it in two pounds of powdered sugar, and add the thin rind of an orange; run this through a sieve, and stir in by degrees the whites of ten eggs, beaten into a froth. Put the bowl with the mixture into an ice pail, let it freeze a little, then stir briskly into it a bottle of wine and a bottle of rum.

TEA PUNCH

Make an infusion of the best green tea, an ounce to a quart of boiling water; put before the fire a silver or other metal bowl, to become quite hot, and then put into it:

One-half pint of good brandy	One-half pint of rum
One-quarter pound of lump sugar	The juice of a large lemon

Set these alight, and pour in the tea gradually, mixing it from time to time with a ladle; it will remain burning for some time, and is to be poured in that state into the glasses; in order to increase the flavor, a few lumps of the sugar should be rubbed over the lemon peel. This punch may be made in a china bowl, but in that case the flame goes off more rapidly.

WEST INDIAN PUNCH

This punch is made the same as brandy punch, but to each glass add a clove or two of preserved ginger, and a little of the syrup.

BARBADOES PUNCH

To each glass of brandy punch, add a tablespoon of guava jelly.

YORKSHIRE PUNCH

Rub off the rind of three lemons on pieces of sugar, put the sugar into a jug, and add to it the thin rind of one lemon and an orange, and the juice of four oranges and of ten lemons, with six glasses of dissolved calf's-foot jelly. Pour two quarts of water over the whole, mixing the materials well; then cover the jug, and keep it on a warm hearth for twenty minutes. Then strain the mixture, and add a pint of clarified syrup, half a pint each of rum and brandy, and a bottle of good orange or lemon shrub.

APPLE PUNCH

Lay in a china bowl slices of apples and lemons alternately, each layer being thickly strewed with powdered sugar. Pour over the fruit, when the bowl is half filled, a bottle of claret; cover, and let it stand six hours. Then pour it through a muslin bag, and send it up immediately.

ALE PUNCH

A quart of mild ale, a glass of white wine, one of brandy, one of capillaire, the juice of a lemon, a roll of the peel pared thin, nutmeg grated on the top, and a bit of toasted bread.

CIDER PUNCH

On the thin rind of half a lemon pour half a pint of sherry; add a quarter of a pound of sugar, the juice of a lemon, a little grated nutmeg, and a bottle of cider; mix it well, and, if possible, place it on ice. Add, before sent in, a glass of brandy, and a few pieces of cucumber rind.

NECTAR PUNCH

Infuse the peel of fifteen lemons in a pint and a half of rum for forty-eight hours; add two quarts of cold water with three pints of rum, exclusive of the pint and a half; also the juice of the lemons, with two quarts of boiling hot milk, and one grated nutmeg; pour the milk on the above, and let it stand twenty-four hours, covered close; add two pounds and a half of loaf sugar; then strain it through a flannel bag till quite fine, and bottle it for use. It is fit to use as soon as bottled.

ORANGE PUNCH

From The Bordeaux Wine and Liquor Guide

The juice of three or four oranges
Three-quarters of a pound of
    lump sugar

The peel of one or two oranges
Three and one-half pints of
    boiling water

Infuse half an hour, strain, add one-half pint of porter; three-fourths to one pint each, rum and brandy (or either alone one and one-half to two pints), and add more warm water and sugar, if desired weaker or sweeter. A liqueur glass of curaçao, noyau, or maraschino improves it. A good lemon punch may be made by substituting lemons instead of oranges.

IMPERIAL RASPBERRY
WHISKEY PUNCH

Five ounces of sweet almonds   Five ounces of bitter almonds

Infuse in boiling water. Then skin, and add one-fourth ounce of powdered cinnamon, one-eighth ounce of powdered cloves, and five ounces of plain syrup. Rub them fine. Boil in seven gallons of water for five minutes; strain and when cool add two gallons of whiskey and one gallon of raspberry syrup.

EL DORADO PUNCH

Use large bar glass

One pony of brandy
One-half pony of Jamaica rum
One-half pony of bourbon
A slice of lemon

One tablespoon of powdered
  sugar dissolved in a little
  water

Fill the tumbler with fine ice, shake well and ornament with berries or small pieces of orange. Serve with a straw.

WEDDING PUNCH

One-half pint of pineapple juice
One pint of lemon juice
One pint of lemon syrup
One bottle of claret or port wine

One-half pint of boiling water
Six grains of vanilla
One grain of ambergris
One pint of strong brandy

Rub the vanilla and ambergris with the sugar in the brandy thoroughly; let it stand in a corked bottle for a few hours, shaking occasionally. Then add the lemon juice, pineapple juice and wine; filter through flannel and, lastly, add the syrup.

METFORD PUNCH

Use large bar glass

One tablespoon of powdered
white sugar dissolved in
a little water
One and one-half glass of
Medford rum

One pony glass of Jamaica rum
Two or three dashes of
lemon juice
One slice of orange
(cut in quarters)

Fill the tumbler with ice, shake well, and dress the top with sliced lime and berries in season. Serve with a straw.

MARASCHINO PUNCH

Use large bar glass

One teaspoon of powdered sugar,
dissolved in a little water
One-half pony glass of
maraschino

One wineglass of brandy
Two dashes of arrack
The juice of half a small
lemon

Fill the tumbler with shaved ice, shake well, ornament with fruit and berries in season, and serve with a straw.

PREPARED PUNCH
AND PUNCH ESSENCES

A glass of punch, with all the etceteras, is an excellent thing; the main difficulty about it is that, outside of a well-appointed bar-room, the necessary ingredients are not usually found ready to hand at the moment when they are indispensable; and, even under the most favorable circumstance, it is not everyone that knows the precise proportions and happy blending of flavors that constitute a perfect glass of punch.

The enlightenment of the present day is full of short cuts to comfort, and all the impediments in the way of enjoying a social glass of punch, compounded according to the latest discoveries of the art, are obviated by having a bottle of the desired nectar in a concentrated essence form, ready brewed in exact proportions, and nothing needed but a moderate supply of hot or cold water, or ice, to adjust it to the correct strength and temperature, and a glass to receive the welcome libation.

The following recipes for concocting the latest and most improved varieties of punch are intended for bottling for ready use.

ESSENCE OF CLARET
WINE PUNCH FOR BOTTLING

Five gallons of claret wine

Three gallons of plain syrup

One pint of tincture of
lemon peel

One ounce of tartaric acid

One and one-half ounce of
tincture of cinnamon

Two and one-half gallons
of spirits

One-half pint of raspberry
juice

One and one-half ounce
of tincture of cloves

First dissolve the tartaric acid in a small portion of the spirits. Mix the tinctures with the remainder of the spirits. Pour the two mixtures together, and add the remaining ingredients.

83

ESSENCE OF KIRSCHWASSER
WINE PUNCH FOR BOTTLING

Take seven gallons of plain syrup

Five gallons of kirschwasser

One and one-half gallons
of lemon juice

Mix them thoroughly together and strain through Canton flannel.

ESSENCE OF ST DOMINIGO PUNCH
FOR BOTTLING

Take ten gallons of arrack
Six gallons of plain syrup
Two ounces of tartaric acid
Five drops of oil of cloves

Ten drops of oil of lemon
Five drops of oil of orange
Five drops of oil of cinnamon
Two ounces of alcohol

First dissolve the tartaric acid in a portion of the arrack, and add it to the remainder. Next cut the oils in the alcohol, add this to the arrack, and lastly add the syrup.

GIN PUNCH FOR BOTTLING

Following General Ford's plan, as already described, for making sherbet, add good gin, in the proper proportions before prescribed; this, bottled and kept in a cool cellar or cistern, will be found an economical and excellent summer drink.

ESSENCE OF BOURBON
WHISKEY PUNCH FOR BOTTLING

Four and one-half gallons
Bourbon whiskey
One-half pint tincture
of lemon peel
One-half pint tincture
of orange peel

Three gallons of plain syrup
Three ounces tincture
of all-spice
Five dessertspoons tincture
of cloves

Mix the ingredients thoroughly with the whiskey, and then add the syrup.

The essence of rum punch may be made by substituting Jamaica or Santa Cruz rum for the whiskey.

ESSENCE OF BRANDY PUNCH
FOR BOTTLING

Five gallons of strong brandy
Three gallons of plain syrup
One-half pint tincture of
lemon peel
One-half pint tincture of
orange peel

Three ounces tincture
of all-spice
One-half wineglass tincture
of cloves

Mix the tinctures with the brandy, and add the syrup.

88

ESSENCE OF ARRACK PUNCH
FOR BOTTLING

One and one-half gallon of
    Batavia arrack
Three gallons of plain syrup

Three gallons of spirits
One-half pint of tincture
    of lemon peel

Mix all together, and it is ready for immediate use.

89

CALIFORNIA MILK PUNCH
FOR BOTTLING

The juice of four lemons
The rind of two lemons
One-half pound of white sugar,
    dissolved in just sufficient
    hot water
One pineapple, peeled, sliced
    and pounded
Six cloves

Twenty coriander seeds
One small stick of cinnamon
One pint of brandy
One pint of Jamaica rum
One gill of Batavia arrack
One cup of strong green tea
One quart of boiling water
One quart of hot milk

Put all the materials in a clean demijohn, the boiling water to be added last; cork this down to prevent evaporation, and allow the ingredients to steep for at least six hours; then add the hot milk and the juice of two more lemons; mix, and filter through a jelly-bag; and when the punch has passed bright, put it away in tight corked bottles.

This punch is intended to be iced for drinking.

If intended for present use filtering is not necessary.

COCKTAILS[9]

The cocktail is a modern invention, and is generally used on fishing and other sporting parties, although some *patients* insist that it is good in the morning as a tonic.

90

BOTTLE COCKTAIL

To make a splendid bottle of brandy cocktail, use the following ingredients:

Two-thirds brandy
One-third water
One pony glass of bitters

One wineglass of gum syrup
One-half pony glass of curaçao

The author has always used this recipe in compounding the above beverage for connoisseurs. Whiskey and gin cocktails, in bottles, may be made by using the above recipe, and substituting those liquors instead of brandy.

91

BRANDY COCKTAIL

Use small bar glass

Three or four dashes of
  gum syrup
Two or three dashes of bitters

One wineglass of brandy
One or two dashes of curaçao

Squeeze lemon peel; fill one-third full of ice, and stir with a spoon.

FANCY BRANDY COCKTAIL

Use small bar glass

This drink is made the same as the brandy cocktail, except that it is strained in a fancy wineglass, and a piece of lemon peel thrown on top, and the edge of the glass moistened with lemon.

IMPROVED BRANDY COCKTAIL

Use ordinary bar glass

Two dashes of bitters
Three dashes of gum syrup
Two dashes of maraschino
One dash of absinthe

One small piece of the yellow
rind of the lemon, twisted
to express the oil
One small wineglass of brandy

Fill glass one-third full of shaved ice, shake well, and strain into a fancy cocktail glass; put the lemon peel in the glass and serve.

The flavor is improved by moistening the edge of the cocktail glass with a piece of lemon.

WHISKEY COCKTAIL

Use small bar glass

Three or four dashes of
    gum syrup
Two dashes of bitters

One wineglass of whiskey,
    and a piece of lemon peel

Fill one-third full of fine ice; shake and strain in a fancy red wineglass.

IMPROVED WHISKEY COCKTAIL

Prepared in the same manner as the Improved Brandy Cocktail, by substituting Bourbon or rye whiskey for the brandy.

GIN COCKTAIL

Use small bar glass

Three of four dashes of
    gum syrup
Two dashes of bitters

One wineglass of gin
One or two dashes of curaçao
One small piece of lemon peel

Fill one-third full of fine ice, shake well, and strain in a glass.

FANCY GIN COCKTAIL

Use small bar glass

This drink is made the same as the gin cocktail, except that it is strained in a fancy wineglass and a piece of lemon peel thrown on top, and the edge of the glass moistened with lemon.

IMPROVED GIN COCKTAIL

Made the same way as the Improved Brandy Cocktail substituting Holland or Old Tom gin for the brandy.

SARATOGA COCKTAIL

Use small bar glass

Two dashes of Angostura bitters One pony of whiskey
One pony of brandy One pony of vermouth

Shake up well with two small lumps of ice; strain into a claret glass, and serve with a quarter of a slice of lemon.

CHAMPAGNE COCKTAIL

Per glass

One-half teaspoon of sugar   One piece of lemon peel
One or two dashes of bitters

Fill tumbler one-third full of broken ice, and fill balance with wine. Shake well and serve.

Use one bottle of champagne to every six large glasses.

JAPANESE COCKTAIL

Use small bar glass

One tablespoon of orgeat syrup   One or two pieces
One-half teaspoon of bitters   of lemon peel
One wineglass of brandy

Fill the tumbler one-third with ice, and stir well with a spoon.

JERSEY COCKTAIL

Use small bar glass

One teaspoon of sugar   One pony glass of absinthe
Two dashes of bitters

Pour about one wineglass of water into the tumbler in a small stream from the ice pitcher, or preferably from an absinthe glass. Shake up *very* thoroughly with ice, and strain into a claret glass.

ABSINTHE COCKTAIL

Use small bar glass

Two dashes of anisette   One pony glass of absinthe
One dash of bitters

Pour about one wineglass of water into the tumbler in a small stream from the ice pitcher, or preferably from an absinthe glass. Shake up very thoroughly with ice, and strain into a claret glass.

FANCY VERMOUTH COCKTAIL

Use small bar glass

Two dashes of bitters   One wineglass of vermouth
Two dashes of maraschino   One-quarter slice of lemon

Fill the glass one-quarter full of shaved ice, shake well and strain into a cocktail glass; garnish with the lemon.

MARTINEZ COCKTAIL[10]

Use small bar glass

One dash of bitters   One wineglass of vermouth
Two dashes of maraschino   Two small lumps of ice
One pony of Old Tom gin

Shake up thoroughly, and strain into a large cocktail glass. Put a quarter of a slice of lemon in the glass, and serve. If the guest prefers it very sweet add two dashes of gum syrup.

SODA COCKTAIL

Use large soda glass

One teaspoon of powdered
   white sugar
Two dashes of bitters

One bottle of plain soda
Three or four small lumps
   of ice

Pour the soda water upon the other ingredients, stir well with a spoon, then remove the ice, and serve.

MORNING GLORY COCKTAIL

Use medium bar glass

Three dashes of gum syrup
Two dashes of curaçao
Two dashes of bitters
One dash of absinthe
One pony of brandy

One pony of whiskey
One piece of lemon peel,
   twisted to express the oil
Two small pieces of ice

Stir thoroughly and remove the ice. Fill the glass with seltzer water or plain soda, and stir with a teaspoon having a little sugar in it.

COFFEE COCKTAIL

Use a large bar glass

One teaspoon powdered
    white sugar
One large wineglass of
    port wine

One fresh egg
One pony of brandy
Two or three lumps of ice

Break the egg into the glass, put in the sugar, and lastly the port wine, brandy and ice. Shake up very thoroughly and strain into a medium bar goblet. Grate a little nutmeg on top before serving.

The name of this drink is a misnomer, as coffee and bitters are not to be found among its ingredients, but it looks like coffee when it has been properly concocted, hence probably its name.

MANHATTAN COCKTAIL

Use small bar glass

Two dashes of curaçao
    or maraschino
One pony of rye whiskey

One wineglass of vermouth
Three dashes of bitters
Two small lumps of ice

Shake up well, and strain into a claret glass. Put a quarter of a slice of lemon in the glass and serve. If the customer prefers it very sweet, use also two dashes of gum syrup.

VERMOUTH COCKTAIL

Use small bar glass

Two dashes of bitters   One-quarter slice of lemon
One wineglass of vermouth

Shake the bitters and vermouth with a small lump of ice, strain in a cocktail glass in which the lemon has been placed. If the customer prefers it very sweet, add two dashes of gum syrup.

PREPARED COCKTAILS
FOR BOTTLING

BRANDY COCKTAIL
FOR BOTTLING

Five gallons of strong brandy
Two gallons of water

One quart of gum syrup
One quart of bitters

Mix thoroughly, and filter through Canton flannel.

BRANDY COCKTAIL
FOR BOTTLING

Another recipe

Take five gallons of spirits
  (70 percent)
Two gallons of water
One quart of gum syrup
One-fourth pint of essence
  of Cognac
One ounce of tincture
  of cloves

One ounce of tincture
  of gentian
Two ounces of tincture
  of orange peel
One-fourth ounce of tincture
  of cardamoms
One-half ounce of tincture
  of licorice root

Mix the essence and tinctures with a portion of the spirits; add the remainder of the ingredients, and color with a sufficient quantity of Solferino and caramel (in equal parts) to give the desired color.

GIN COCKTAIL
FOR BOTTLING

Five gallons of gin
Two gallons of water
Two ounces of tincture of
    orange peel
Seven ounces of tincture
    of gentian

One quart of gum syrup
One-half ounce of tincture
    of cardamoms
One-half ounce of tincture
    of orange peel

Mix them together, and give the desired color with Solferino and caramel, in equal proportions.

BOURBON COCKTAIL
FOR BOTTLING

Five gallons of Bourbon
Two gallons of water
Two ounces of tincture
    of orange peel
One ounce of tincture
    of lemon peel

One quart of gum syrup
One ounce of tincture
    of gentian
One-half ounce of tincture
    of cardamoms

Mix these ingredients thoroughly, and color with Solferino and caramel, in equal proportions.

CRUSTA

The crusta is an improvement on the cocktail, and is said to have been invented by Santina, a celebrated Spanish caterer.

115

BRANDY CRUSTA

Use small bar glass

Crusta is made just the same as a fancy cocktail, with a little lemon juice and a small lump of ice added. First, mix the ingredients in a small tumbler, then take a fancy red wineglass, rub a sliced lemon around the rim of the same, and dip it in pulverized white sugar, so that the sugar will adhere to the edge of the glass. Pare half a lemon the same as you would an apple (all in one piece) so that the paring will fit in the wineglass, and strain the crusta from the tumbler into it. Then smile.

116

WHISKEY CRUSTA

Use small bar glass

The whiskey crusta is made the same as the brandy crusta, using whiskey instead of brandy.

117

GIN CRUSTA

Use small bar glass

Gin crusta is made like the brandy crusta, using gin instead of brandy.

FANCY DRINKS

The following miscellaneous collection of fancy beverages embraces a number of French, Spanish, English, Russian, Italian, German and American recipes. Many of them are rather troublesome to prepare, and some of them, which we have tried, have not yielded the satisfaction expected or desired.

118

POUSSE L'AMOUR

Use a sherry glass

One-half glass of maraschino	Yolk of one egg
One tablespoon of fine old brandy	Sufficient vanilla cordial to surround the egg

First, pour in the maraschino, then introduce the yolk with a spoon, without disturbing the maraschino, next carefully surround the egg with vanilla cordial, and lastly put the brandy on top.

In making a pousse of any kind the greatest care should be observed to keep all the ingredients composing it separate. This may best be accomplished by pouring the different materials from a sherry wine glass.

It requires a steady hand and careful manipulation to succeed in making a perfect pousse.

SANTINA'S POUSSE-CAFÉ

Use small wineglass

This delicious drink is from a recipe by Santina, proprietor of Santina's Saloon, a celebrated Spanish café in New Orleans.

One-third brandy (Cognac)   One-third curaçao
One-third maraschino

Mix well.

PARISIAN POUSSE-CAFÉ

Use small wineglass

Two-fifths curaçao   One-fifth chartreuse
Two-fifths kirschwasser

This is a celebrated Parisian drink.

FAIVRE'S POUSSE-CAFÉ

Use small wineglass

One-third Parisian pousse-café
  (as above)

One-third kirschwasser
One-third curaçao

This celebrated drink is from the recipe of M. Faivre, a popular proprietor of a 'French Saloon' in New York.

SARATOGA POUSSE-CAFÉ

Use small wineglass

One-fifth curaçao
One-fifth benedictine
One-fifth raspberry syrup

Two-fifths fine old brandy
One teaspoon of vanilla
  cordial on top

In making this pousse, the same precautions must be observed as directed in the preceding recipes.

123

BRANDY CHAMPERELLE

Use small wineglass

One-third brandy   One-third curaçao
One-third bitters

This is a delicious French café drink.

124

BRANDY SCAFFA

Use wineglass

One-half brandy   Two dashes of bitters
One-half Maraschino

CLARET AND CHAMPAGNE CUP,
À LA BRUNOW

For a party of twenty

The following claret and champagne cup ought, from its excellence, to be called the Nectar of the Czar, as it is so highly appreciated in Russia, where for many years it has enjoyed a high reputation amongst the aristocracy of the Muscovite empire. Proportions:

Three bottles of claret
Two-thirds pint of curaçao
One pint of sherry
One-half pint of brandy
Two wineglasses of ratafia*
   of raspberries

Some sprigs of green balm,
   and of borage, and a small
   piece of rind of cucumber
Two bottles of German
   seltzer water
Three bottles of soda water

Stir this together, and sweeten with capillaire or pounded sugar, until it ferments; let it stand one hour, strain it, and ice it well; it is then fit for use. Serve in small glasses.

The same for champagne cup: champagne instead of claret; noyau instead of ratafia.

This quantity is for an evening party of twenty persons. For a smaller number reduce the proportions.

---

* Every liqueur made by infusion is called ratafia. That is, when the spirit is made to imbibe thoroughly the aromatic flavor and color of the fruit steeped in it; when this has taken place, the liqueur is drawn off. Sugar is added, and it is then filtered and bottled.

BALAKLAVA NECTAR

Soyer's Recipe
For a party of fifteen

Thinly peel the rind of half a lemon, shred it fine, and put it in a punch bowl; add two tablespoons of crushed sugar, and the juice of two lemons, the half of a small cucumber sliced thin, with the peel on; toss it up several times, then add two bottles of soda water, two of claret, one of champagne, stir well together, and serve.

CRIMEAN CUP, À LA MORMORA

From a recipe by the celebrated Soyer
For a party of thirty

One quart of syrup of orgeat
One pint of Cognac brandy
One-half pint of maraschino
One-half pint of
  Jamaica rum

Two bottles of champagne
Two bottles of soda water
Six ounces of sugar
Four middling-sized
  lemons

Thinly peel the lemons, and place the rind in a bowl with the sugar; macerate them well for a minute or two, in order to extract the flavor from the lemon. Next squeeze the juice of the lemons upon this, add two bottles of soda water, and stir well till the sugar is dissolved; pour in the syrup of orgeat, and whip the mixture well with an egg-whisk, in order to whiten the composition. Then add the brandy, rum and maraschino, strain the whole into the punchbowl, and just before serving add the champagne, which should be well iced. While adding the champagne, stir well with the ladle; this will render the cup creamy and mellow.

Half the quantity given here, or even less, may be made, this recipe being for a party of thirty.

128

CRIMEAN CUP, À LA WYNDHAM

For a party of five

Thinly peel the rind of half an orange, put it into a bowl, with a tablespoon of crushed sugar, and macerate with the ladle for a minute; then add one large wineglass of maraschino, half one of Cognac, half one of curaçao. Mix well together, pour in two bottles of soda water, and one of champagne, during which time work it up and down with the punch ladle, and it is ready.

Half a pound of pure ice is a great improvement.

129

CLARET CUP

Bott a bottle of thin claret; add half a pint of cold water, a tablespoon of finely powdered sugar, and a teaspoon of cinnamon, cloves, and all-spice, finely powdered and mixed together. Mix all well together, then add half the thin rind of a small lemon. This is a delicious summer beverage for evening parties.

PORTER CUP

Mix in a tankard or covered jug a bottle of porter, and an equal quantity of table ale; pour in a glass of brandy, a dessertspoon of syrup of ginger, add three or four lumps of sugar, and half a nutmeg grated; cover it down, and expose it to the cold for half an hour; just before sending it to table, stir in a teaspoon of carbonate of soda. Add the fresh cut rind of a cucumber.

CHAMPAGNE, HOCK OR CHABLIS CUP

À la Goodriche

Dissolve four or five lumps of sugar in a quarter of a pint of boiling water, with a little very thin lemon peel; let it stand a quarter of an hour; add one bottle of the above wines, and a sprig of verbena, a small glass of sherry, half a pint of water. Mix well, and let stand half an hour; strain, and ice it well.

132

CIDER NECTAR

À la Harold Littledale

One quart of cider   One glass of sherry
One bottle of soda water   One small glass of brandy

Juice of half a lemon, peel of quarter of a lemon; sugar and nutmeg to taste; a sprig of verbena. Flavor it to taste with extract of pineapple. Strain, and ice it all well. This is a delicious beverage, and only requires to be tasted to be appreciated.

133

BOTTLED VELVET

À la John Bayley

A bottle of Moselle, half a pint of sherry, the peel of a lemon, not too much, so as to have the flavor predominate; two tablespoons of sugar; add a sprig of verbena; all must be well mixed, and then strained and iced.

TOM AND JERRY

Use punch bowl for the mixture

Five pounds of sugar
One-half small glass of
    Jamaica rum
One and one-half teaspoon
    of ground cinnamon

Twelve eggs
One-half teaspoon ground
    cloves
One-half teaspoon ground
    all-spice

Beat the whites of the eggs to a stiff froth, and the yolks until they are as thin as water, then mix together and add the spice and rum; thicken with sugar until the mixture attains the consistency of a light batter.

To deal out Tom and Jerry to customers:
Take a small bar glass, and to one tablespoon of the above mixture, add one wineglass of brandy, and fill the glass with boiling water; grate a little nutmeg on top.

Adepts at the bar, in serving Tom and Jerry, sometimes adopt a mixture of one-half brandy, one-fourth Jamaica rum, and one-fourth Santa Cruz rum, instead of brandy plain. This compound is usually mixed and kept in a bottle, and a wineglassful is used to each tumbler of Tom and Jerry.

NB. A teaspoon of cream of tartar, or about as much carbonate of soda as you can get on a dime, will prevent the sugar from settling to the bottom of the mixture.

This drink is sometimes called *Copenhagen*, and sometimes *Jerry Thomas*.

WHITE TIGER'S MILK

From a recipe in the possession of Thomas Dunn English, Esq.[II]

One-half gill of applejack
One-half gill of peach brandy
One-half teaspoon of aromatic
   tincture
One quart of pure milk

Sweeten with white sugar
   to taste
The white of an egg beaten
   to a stiff foam

Pour in the mixed liquors to the milk, stirring all the while till it is well mixed, then sprinkle with nutmeg.

The above recipe is sufficient to make a full quart of 'white tiger's milk'; if more is wanted, you can increase the above proportions. If you want to prepare this beverage for a party of twenty, use one gallon of milk to one pint of applejack, etc.

WHITE LION

Use small bar glass

One and one-half teaspoons of
   pulverized white sugar
One-half a lime
   (squeeze out the juice and
   put the rind in the glass)

One wineglass of Santa Cruz
   rum
One-half teaspoon of curaçao
One-half teaspoon of
   raspberry syrup

Mix well, ornament with berries in season, and cool with shaved ice.

BISHOP

À la Prusse

A favorite beverage, made with claret or port. It is prepared as follows: roast four good-sized bitter oranges till they are of a pale-brown color, lay them in a tureen, and put over them half a pound of pounded loaf sugar, and three glasses of claret; place the cover on the tureen and let it stand till the next day. When required for use, put the tureen into a pan of boiling water, press the oranges with a spoon, and run the juice through a sieve; then boil the remainder of the bottle of claret, taking care that it does not burn; add it to the strained juice, and serve it warm in glasses. Port wine will answer the purpose as well as claret. Bishop is sometimes made with the above materials, substituting lemons instead of oranges, but this is not often done when claret is used.

138

BISHOP

Use large soda glass

One teaspoon of powdered white sugar dissolved in one wineglass of water
Two thin slices of lemon

Two dashes of Jamaica rum
Two or three small lumps of ice

Fill the glass with claret or red Burgundy, shake up well, and remove the ice before serving.

ENGLISH BISHOP

Stick an orange full of cloves, and roast it before a fire. When brown enough, cut it in quarters, and pour over it a quart of hot port wine, add sugar to the taste; let the mixture simmer for half an hour.

ARCHBISHOP

The same as Bishop, substituting claret for the port.

CARDINAL

Same as above, substituting champagne for claret.

POPE

Same as above, substituting Burgundy for champagne.

143

PROTESTANT BISHOP

Four tablespoons of
  white sugar
Two tumblers of water
One lemon, in slices
Ice

One bottle of claret
Four tablespoons
  of Santa Cruz
  or Jamaica rum

144

KNICKERBOCKER

Use small glass

One-half a lime, or lemon;
  squeeze out the juice,
  and put the rind and juice
  in the glass
One-half teaspoon of curaçao

Two teaspoons of raspberry
  syrup
One wineglass Santa Cruz
  rum

Cool with shaved ice; shake up well, and ornament with berries in season. If this is not sweet enough, put in a little more raspberry syrup.

145

RUMFUSTIAN

This is the singular name bestowed upon a drink very much in vogue with English sportsmen, after their return from a day's shooting, and is concocted thus:

The yolks of a dozen eggs are well whisked up, and put into a quart of strong beer; to this is added a pint of gin; a bottle of sherry is put into a saucepan, with a stick of cinnamon, a nutmeg grated, a dozen large lumps of sugar and the rind of a lemon peeled very thin; when the wine boils, it is poured upon the gin and beer, and the whole drunk hot.

146

ENGLISH CURAÇAO

Cut away the peel of oranges very thin, until you have obtained half a dozen ounces of it; put these in a quart bottle, and then pour in a pint of genuine whiskey. Cork the bottle down tightly, and let the rind remain infused for ten or twelve days, giving the bottle a good shake as often as you have an opportunity for so doing; at the end of this period, take out the orange peel, and fill the bottle with clarified syrup, shake it well with the spirit, and let it remain for three days. Pour a teacupful of the liqueur into a mortar, and beat up a drachm of powdered alum, and an equal quantity of carbonate of potash; pour this, when well mixed, into the bottle, shake it well, and in a week you will find the curaçao perfectly transparent, and equal in flavor to that imported from Malines, or any other place in the universe.

147

ITALIAN LEMONADE

Pare and press two dozen lemons; pour the juice on the peels, and let it remain on them all night; in the morning add two pounds of loaf sugar, a quart of good sherry, and three quarts of boiling water. Mix well, add a quart of boiling milk, and strain it through a jelly-bag till clear.

148

QUINCE LIQUEUR

Two quarts of quince juice
Four quarts of Cognac brandy
Two and one-half pounds of
  white sugar

Twelve ounces of bitter
  almonds, bruised
One pound of coriander seeds
Thirty-six cloves

Grate a sufficient number of quinces to make two quarts of juice, and squeeze them through a jelly-bag. Mix the ingredients all together, and put them in a demijohn, and shake them well every day for ten days. Then strain the liquid through a jelly-bag till it is perfectly clear, and bottle for use. This is a delightful liqueur, and can be relied upon, as it is from a recipe in the possession of a lady who is famous for concocting delicious potations.

149

WEST INDIA COUPEREE

Use large soda glass

One and one-half pony glass
  of brandy
One pony glass maraschino
  or curaçao

Fill the glass one-third full
  of vanilla ice cream

Mix thoroughly, and fill the glass nearly full with plain soda. Grate a little nutmeg on top, and serve.

150

SLEEPER

One gill of old rum
One ounce of sugar
Two fresh raw eggs
One-half pint of water

Six cloves
Six coriander seeds
One lemon

Boil the cloves and coriander, with a bit of cinnamon in the water; mix together the rum and sugar, the yolks of the eggs and the juice of half the lemon; whisk them all together, and strain into a tumbler.

151

BADMINTON[12]

Peel half of a middle-sized cucumber, and put it into a silver cup, with four ounces of powdered sugar, a little nutmeg, and a bottle of claret. When the sugar is thoroughly dissolved, pour in a bottle of soda water, and it is fit for use.

LOCOMOTIVE

Use large bar glass

One tablespoon of genuine
  honey
The yolk of a fresh raw egg

Three dashes of curaçao
One claret glass of red
  Burgundy

Heat the wine in a *thoroughly clean* saucepan until it boils, then pour it *gradually upon the other ingredients* (which, previously, should have been thoroughly beaten together in a mug or pitcher), whisking and stirring the materials all the while, in order to prevent the egg from curdling. Pour the mixture into a large bar glass, powder a little cinnamon on top, and add two or three cloves before serving.

This seems like taking too much trouble just to make one glass of Locomotive. The following proportions of ingredients make four nice glasses:

Two ounces of honey
Two pony glasses of high
  red Burgundy

A few drops of essence
  of cloves

Proceed as directed above, and serve in large goblets previously heated.

SARATOGA BRACE UP

Use large bar glass

One tablespoon of fine
  white sugar
Two dashes of bitters
Four dashes of lemon or
  lime juice

Two dashes of absinthe
One fresh egg
One wineglass of brandy
Two or three small lumps
  of ice

Shake up thoroughly, strain into another glass, and fill it up with seltzer water.

WHITE PLUSH

Use small bar glass

Hand a bottle of Bourbon or rye whiskey to the customer and let him help himself.

Fill up the glass with fresh milk.

A curious story about the origin of this drink is thus told by the *New York Herald:*

'There are always some mixed drinks that are standbys, and are always popular, such as cocktails, punches and juleps; but every little while there will be a new racket sprung on the public that will have a great run for a time, and then get knocked out by another. About a month ago white plush got its star in this way: there was a country buyer down from New England somewhere, and a party of dry goods men were trying to make it pleasant for him. So they took him into a swell barroom down town, and were going to open sour wine. Same old story, you know; get him full as a balloon and then work him for a big order. It turned out that this countryman was not such a flat as they thought him. Though he had been swigging barrels of hard cider and smuggled Canada whiskey for the last twenty years, he pleaded the temperance business on them; said he never drank, and he guessed he'd just take a glass of water if they'd get him one, as he was kinder thirsty walkin' round so much. Well, that was a setback for the boys. They knew he had lots of money to spend, and he was one of those unapproachable ducks that have got to be wormed up before you can do anything with them.

'"Oh, take something," they said, "take some milk."

'"Well, I guess a glass of milk would go sorter good," said he.

'Someone suggested kumyss and told him what it was. As they did not have any kumyss in the place they gave him some milk and seltzer. That's about the same thing. One of the boys gave the bartender a wink and he put a dash of whiskey in it. The old man did not get on to it at all. He thought it was the seltzer that flavored it. The next round the seltzer was left out altogether and more whiskey put in. They kept on giving it to him until he got pretty well set up. It's a very insidious and seductive drink. Pretty soon the countryman got funny and tipped his glass over on the table. As it spread around he said:

'"Gosh, it looks like white plush, don't it?"

'"So it does," said the boys. "Give the gentleman another yard of white plush, here," and the name has stuck to it ever since.'

SHANDY GAFF

Use large bar glass, or mug

Fill the glass half full of ale, and the remaining half with Irish ginger ale.

In England, where this drink has its origin, it is made with Bass' ale and ginger ale, half and half.

HALF AND HALF

Use metal or stone bar mug

Mix half old and new ale together.

This is the American method.

'ARF AND 'ARF

Use metal or stone bar mug

Mix porter and stout, with ale in equal quantities, or in proportions to suit the taste.

This is the English method, and usually, 'draw it mild, Mary, the ale first.'

MISCELLANEOUS DRINKS

158

BLUE BLAZER[13]

Use two large silver-plated mugs, with handles

One wineglass of Scotch whiskey   One wineglass of boiling water

Put the whiskey and the boiling water in one mug, ignite the liquid with fire, and while blazing mix both ingredients by pouring them four or five times from one mug to the other. If well done, this will have the appearance of a continued stream of liquid fire.

Sweeten with one teaspoon of pulverized white sugar, and serve in a small bar tumbler, with a piece of lemon peel.

The 'Blue Blazer' does not have a very euphonious or classic name, but it tastes better to the palate than it sounds to the ear. A beholder gazing for the first time upon an experienced artist compounding this beverage, would naturally come to the conclusion that it was a nectar for Pluto rather than Bacchus. The novice in mixing this beverage should be careful not to scald himself. To become proficient in throwing the liquid from one mug to the other, it will be necessary to practise for some time with cold water.

JERRY THOMAS'
OWN DECANTER BITTERS

One-fourth pound of raisins
Two ounces of cinnamon
One ounce snakeroot
One lemon and one orange
   cut in slices
One ounce of cloves

One ounce of all-spice
Fill decanter with Santa
   Cruz rum
Bottle and serve out in pony
   glasses

As fast as the bitters is used, fill up again with rum.

BURNT BRANDY AND PEACH

Use small bar glass

One wineglass of Cognac and
   one-half tablespoon of
   white sugar, burnt in a saucer
   or plate

Two or three slices of dried
   peaches
Place the dried fruit in a glass
   and pour the liquid over
   them

This drink is very popular in the Southern states, where it is sometimes used as a cure for diarrhoea.

BLACK STRIPE

Use small bar glass

One wineglass of Santa Cruz   One tablespoon of molasses
rum

This drink can either be made in summer or winter: if in the former season, mix in one tablespoon of water, and cool with shaved ice; if in the latter, fill up the tumbler with boiling water. Grate a little nutmeg on top.

PEACH AND HONEY

Use small bar glass

One teaspoon of honey   One wineglass of peach brandy

Stir with a spoon.

GIN AND PINE

Use wineglass

Split a piece of the heart of a green pine log into fine splints, about the size of a cedar lead-pencil; take two ounces of the same and put into a quart decanter, and fill the decanter with gin.

Let the pine soak for two hours, and the gin will be ready to serve.

GIN AND TANSY

Use wineglass

Fill a quart decanter one-third full of tansy, and pour in gin to fill up the balance, one-third tansy to two-thirds gin. Serve to customers in a wineglass.

GIN AND WORMWOOD

Use small bar glass

Put three or four sprigs of wormwood into a quart decanter, and fill up with gin.

The above three drinks are not much used except in small country villages.

HOT SPICED RUM

Use small bar glass

One teaspoon of sugar
One teaspoon of mixed spiced
  (all-spice and cloves)

One wineglass of Jamaica rum
One piece of butter as large
  as half a chestnut

Fill the tumbler with hot water.

HOT RUM

Use small bar glass

This drink is made the same as the hot spiced rum, omitting the spices, and grating a little nutmeg on top.

STONE FENCE

Use large bar glass

One wineglass of Bourbon
  whiskey

Two or three small lumps
  of ice

Fill up the glass with sweet cider.

RHINE WINE
AND SELTZER WATER

Use large bar glass

Fill large bar glass half full of Rhine wine, and fill balance with seltzer water. This is a German drink, and is not very likely to be called for at an American bar.

BRANDY STRAIGHT

Use small bar glass

In serving this drink you simply put a piece of ice in a tumbler, and hand it to your customer, with the bottle of brandy. This is very safe for a steady drink, but though a *straight* beverage, it is often used on a *bender*.

GIN STRAIGHT

Use small bar glass

Same as brandy straight, substituting gin for brandy.

SPLIT SODA AND BRANDY

Use medium bar glass

One pony glass of brandy   One small lump of ice

Add one-half of a bottle of plain soda water.

BRANDY AND GINGER ALE

Use large soda-water glass

One wineglass of brandy   Two or three small lumps of ice

Fill up the glass with Irish ginger ale.

PONY BRANDY

Use pony glass

Fill the pony glass with brandy, and hand it to your customer.

BRANDY AND SODA

Sometimes called Stone Wall

Use large bar glass

One wineglass of Cognac brandy   One-third glass of fine ice

Fill up with plain soda.

BRANDY AND GUM

Use small bar glass

Same as brandy straight, with one dash of gum syrup.

SHERRY AND EGG

Use small bar glass

One wineglass of sherry   One egg

Mix well.

178

SHERRY AND BITTERS

One wineglass of sherry   One dash of bitters

Mix well.

179

SHERRY AND ICE

Use small bar glass

Put two lumps of ice in a glass, and fill with wine.

180

ABSINTHE

Use small bar glass

One wineglass of absinthe

Pour water, drop by drop, until the glass is full. Never use a spoon.

FRENCH METHOD OF
SERVING ABSINTHE

Use a champagne glass standing in a bowl

One pony glass of absinthe

Let the water drip, as directed in the preceding recipe, until the glass is full, and a very little runs over into the bowl.

ABSINTHE AND WATER

An improved method

One pony glass of absinthe

Fill an absinthe glass (which is a glass made purposefully with a hole in the bottom) with shaved ice and water. Raise this glass about one foot above the tumbler containing the absinthe, and let sufficient water drip into it.

EGGNOGS

Eggnog is a beverage of American origin, but it has a popularity that is cosmopolitan. At the South it is almost indispensable at Christmas time, and at the North it is a favorite at all seasons.

In Scotland they call eggnog 'auld man's milk'.

183

EGGNOG

Use large bar glass

One tablespoon of fine sugar, dissolved with one tablespoon of cold water
One egg
One-third tumblerful of milk
One wineglass of Cognac brandy
One-half wineglass Santa Cruz rum

Fill the tumbler one-fourth full with shaved ice, shake the ingredients together until they are *thoroughly mixed together*, and grate a little nutmeg on top. Every well-ordered bar has a tin eggnog shaker, which is a great aid in making this beverage.

184

HOT EGGNOG

Use large bar glass

This drink is very popular in California, and is made in precisely the same manner as the cold eggnog above, except that you must use boiling water instead of ice.

EGGNOG

For a party of twenty

One dozen eggs

Two quarts of brandy

One pint of Santa Cruz rum

Two gallons of milk

One and one-half pounds
white sugar

Separate the whites of the eggs from the yolks, beat them separately with an egg-beater until the yolks are well cut up, and the whites assume a light fleecy appearance. Mix all the ingredients (except the whites of the eggs) in a large punch bowl, then let the whites float on top, and ornament with colored sugars. Cool in a tub of ice, and serve.

BALTIMORE EGGNOG

For a party of fifteen

Take the yellow of sixteen eggs and twelve tablespoons of pulverized loaf sugar, and beat them to the consistency of cream; to this add two-thirds of a nutmeg grated, and beat well together; then mix in half a pint of good brandy or Jamaica rum, and two wineglasses of Madeira wine. Have ready the whites of the eggs, beaten to a stiff froth, and beat them into the above described mixture. When this is all done, stir in six pints of good rich milk. There is no heat used.

Eggnog made in this manner is digestible, and will not cause headache. It makes an excellent drink for debilitated persons, and a nourishing diet for consumptives.

GENERAL HARRISON'S EGGNOG[14]

Use large bar glass

One egg
One and one-half teaspoon
of sugar

Fill the tumbler with cider,
and shake well
Two or three small lumps of ice

This is a splendid drink, and is very popular on the Mississippi river. It was General Harrison's favorite beverage.

SHERRY EGGNOG

One tablespoon of white sugar   One egg
Two wineglasses of sherry

Dissolve the sugar with a little water; break the yolk of the egg in a large glass; put in one-quarter tumblerful of broken ice; fill with milk, and shake up until the egg is thoroughly mixed with the other ingredients, then grate a little nutmeg on top, and quaff the nectar cup.

JULEPS

The julep is peculiarly an American beverage, and in the Southern states is more popular than any other. It was introduced into England by Captain Marryatt, where it is now quite a favorite. The gallant captain seems to have had a penchant for the nectareous drink, and published the recipe in his work on America. We give it in his own words: 'I must descant a little upon the mint julep, as it is, with the thermometer at 100 degrees, one of the most delightful and insinuating potations that ever was invented, and may be drunk with equal satisfaction when the thermometer is as low as 70 degrees. There are many varieties, such as those composed of claret, Madeira, etc.; but the ingredients of the real mint julep are as follows. I learned how to make them, and succeeded pretty well. Put into a tumbler about a dozen sprigs of the tender shoots of mint, upon them put a spoonful of white sugar, and equal proportions of peach and common brandy, so as to fill it up one-third, or perhaps a little less. Then take rasped or pounded ice, and fill up the tumbler. Epicures rub the lips of the tumbler with a piece of fresh pineapple, and the tumbler itself is very often encrusted outside with stalactites of ice. As the ice melts, you drink. I once overheard two ladies talking in the next room to me, and one of them said, "Well, if I have a weakness for any one thing, it is for a mint julep!" – a very amiable weakness, and proving her good sense and good taste. They are, in fact, like the American ladies, irresistible.'

A Georgia paper recently speaking on this subject says:

'Probably the old-fashioned julep is in its decadence as a public drink, but it does not follow that the art of constructing this famous Southern refresher is lost. On the contrary, we have knowledge of several old-fashioned gardens where the mint-bed under the southern wall still blooms luxuriantly; where white fingers of household angels come every day about this time of the year and pluck a few sprays of the aromatic herb to build a julep for poor old shaky grandpa, who sits in the shady corner of the veranda with his feet on the rail and his head busy with the olden days.

In such a household the art is still preserved. With her sleeves rolled up, the rosy granddaughter stirs sugar in a couple of tablespoons of sparkling water, packs crushed ice to the top of the heavy cut-glass goblet, pours in the mellow whiskey until an overthrow threatens and daintily thrusts the mint sprays into the crevices. And the old man, rousing from his dreams, blesses the vision which seems to rise up from the buried days of his youth, and with his gay nose nestling peacefully in the nosegay at the summit of his midday refresher, quaffs the icy drink, and with a long-drawn sigh of relief sinks back to dream again until the dinner bell sounds its hospitable summons. The mint julep still lives, but it is by no means fashionable. Somehow the idea has gotten abroad that the mint ought to be crushed and shaken up with water and whiskey in equal proportions. No man can fall in love with such a mixture. Poor juleps have ruined the reputation of the South's most famous drink.'

189

REAL GEORGIA MINT JULEP

Use large bar glass

One teaspoon of white powdered sugar

Three-quarters wineglass of Cognac brandy

Three-quarters wineglass of peach brandy

About twelve sprigs of the tender shoots of mint

Put the mint in the tumbler, add the sugar, having previously dissolved it in a little water, then the brandy, and lastly, fill up the glass with shaved ice. Stir with a spoon but do not crush the mint. This is the genuine method of concocting a Southern mint julep, but whiskey may be substituted for brandy if preferred.

MINT JULEP

Use large bar glass

One tablespoon of white pulverized sugar	Two and one-half tablespoons of water; mix well with a spoon

Take three or four sprigs of fresh mint, and press them well in the sugar and water, until the flavor of the mint is extracted; add one and a half wineglasses of Cognac brandy, and fill the glass with fine shaved ice, then draw out the sprigs of mint and insert them in the ice with the stems downward, so that the leaves will be above, in the shape of a bouquet; arrange berries, and small pieces of sliced orange on top in a tasty manner, dash with Jamaica rum, and sprinkle white sugar on top. Place a straw tastily, and you have a julep that is fit for an emperor.

BRANDY JULEP

Use large bar glass

The brandy julep is made with the same ingredients as the mint julep, omitting the fancy fixings.

GIN JULEP

Use large bar glass

The gin julep is made with the same ingredients as the mint julep, omitting the fancy fixings.

WHISKEY JULEP

Use large bar glass

The whiskey julep is made the same as the mint julep, omitting all fruits and berries.

PINEAPPLE JULEP

For a party of five

Peel, slice and cut up a ripe pineapple into a glass bowl, add the juice of two oranges, a gill of raspberry syrup, a gill of maraschino, a gill of old gin, a bottle of sparkling Moselle, and about a pound of pure ice in shaves; mix, ornament with berries in season, and serve in flat glasses.

NEGUS

This is an English beverage and derives its name from Colonel Negus,[15] who is said to have invented it. It may be made of sherry or any other sweet wine, but it is more usually made of port.

195

PORT WINE NEGUS

To every pint of port wine allow:

One quart of boiling water	One lemon
One-quarter pound of loaf sugar	Grated nutmeg to taste

Put the wine into a jug, rub some lumps of sugar (equal to one-fourth pound) on the lemon rind until all the yellow part of the skin is absorbed, then squeeze the juice and strain it. Add the sugar and lemon juice to the port wine, with the grated nutmeg, cover the jug, and when the beverage has cooled a little, it will be fit for use.

PORT WINE NEGUS

Another recipe

One wineglass of port wine   One teaspoon of sugar

Fill tumbler one-third full with hot water.

SODA NEGUS

A most refreshing and elegant beverage, particularly for those who do not take punch or grog after supper, is thus made:

Put half a pint of port wine, with four lumps of sugar, three cloves, and enough grated nutmeg to cover a shilling, into a saucepan; warm it well, but do not suffer it to boil; pour it into a bowl or jug, and upon the warm wine decant a bottle of soda water. You will have an effervescing and delicious negus by this means.

MULLS

198

MULLED WINE
WITHOUT EGGS

To every pint of wine allow:

One small tumblerful of water   Sugar and spice to taste

In making preparations like the above, it is very difficult to give the exact proportions of ingredients like sugar and spice, as what quantity might suit one person would be to another quite distasteful. Boil the spice in the water until the flavor is extracted, then add the wine and sugar, and bring the whole to the boiling point, then serve with strips of crisp, dry toast or with biscuit. The spices usually used for mulled wine are cloves, grated nutmeg, and cinnamon or mace. Any kind of wine may be mulled, but port or claret are those usually selected for that purpose, and the latter requires a large proportion of sugar. The vessel that the wine is boiled in must be delicately clean.

MULLED WINE,
WITH EGGS

Use punch bowl

Nine fresh eggs	One quart either of port,
Four tablespoons of powdered	claret, or red Burgundy wine
white sugar	Grated nutmeg to taste
One pint of water	

Beat up the whites and the yolks of the eggs separately, the sugar with the yolks. Pour into a *delicately clean* skillet the wine and half a pint of water, set this in the bowl with the balance of the water and beat them together thoroughly. When the wine boils pour it on the mixture in the bowl, add the nutmeg, and stir in rapidly.

Be careful not to *pour the mixture into the wine*, or the eggs will curdle.

Some persons may prefer more sugar, and the addition of a little all-spice, but this is a matter of taste.

MULLED WINE

With the whites of eggs

Dissolve one pound of sugar in two pints of hot water, to which add two and a half pints of good sherry wine, and let the mixture be set upon the fire until it is almost ready to boil. Meantime beat up the whites of the eggs to a froth, and pour into them the hot mixture, stirring rapidly. Add a little nutmeg.

MULLED WINE

First, my dear madam, you must take
Nine eggs, which carefully you'll break –
Into a bowl you'll drop the white,
The yolks into another by it.
Let Betsy beat the whites with switch,
Till they appear quite frothed and rich –
Another hand the yolks must beat
With sugar, which will make them sweet;
Three or four spoonfuls maybe'll do,
Though some, perhaps, would take but two.
Into a skillet next you'll pour
A bottle of good wine, or more –
Put half a pint of water, too,
Or it may prove too strong for you;
And while the eggs (by two) are beating,
The wine and water may be heating;
But when it comes to boiling heat,
The yolks and whites together beat
With half a pint of water more –
Mixing them well, then gently pour
Into the skillet with the wine,
And stir it briskly all the time.
Then pour it off into a pitcher;
Grate nutmeg in to make it richer.
Then drink it hot, for he's a fool,
Who lets such precious liquor cool.

MULLED CLARET

À la Lord Saltoun

Peel one lemon fine, add to it some white pounded sugar; pour over one glass of sherry, then add a bottle of claret (*vin ordinaire* is the best) and sugar to taste; add a sprig of verbena, one bottle of soda water, and nutmeg, if you like it. For cup, strain and ice it well. For mull, heat it and serve it hot.

MULLED CIDER

Cider may be mulled in precisely the same manner as recommended in the recipe for mulled wine with eggs, omitting the water, and using twice the quantity of cider for the same number of eggs.

FLIPS

204

RUM FLIP

Which Dibdin[16] has immortalized as the favorite beverage of sailors (although we believe they seldom indulge in it) – is made by adding a gill of rum to the beer, or substituting rum and water, when malt liquor cannot be procured. The essential in flips of all sorts is to produce the smoothness by repeated pouring back and forward between two vessels, and beating up the eggs well in the first instance; the sweetening and spices according to taste.

205

RUM FLIP

Another recipe

Keep grated ginger and nutmeg with a little fine dried lemon peel, rubbed together in a mortar.

To make a quart of flip: put the ale on the fire to warm, and beat up three or four eggs with four ounces of moist sugar, a teaspoon of grated nutmeg or ginger, and a gill of good old rum or brandy. When the ale is near to boil, put it into one pitcher, and the rum and eggs, etc., into another; turn it from one pitcher to another till it is as smooth as cream.

COLD RUM FLIP

Use large bar glass

One teaspoon of powdered
   sugar, dissolved in a
   little water
Two or three lumps of ice

One wineglass of Jamaica
   rum
One fresh egg

Shake up thoroughly, strain in a medium glass, and grate a little nutmeg on top.

HOT ENGLISH
RUM FLIP

One quart

One quart of ale
One gill of rum
Four raw fresh eggs

Four ounces of moist sugar
One teaspoon of grated
   nutmeg (or ginger)

Heat the ale in a saucepan; beat up the eggs and sugar, add the nutmeg and rum, and put it all in a pitcher. When the ale is near to the boil, put it in another pitcher, pour it very gradually in the pitcher containing the eggs, etc., stirring all the while very briskly to prevent the eggs from curdling, then pour the contents of the two pitchers from one to the other until the mixture is as smooth as cream.

208

BRANDY FLIP

Use small bar glass

One teaspoon of sugar   One wineglass of brandy

Fill the tumbler one-third full of hot water, mix, and place a toasted cracker on top, and grate nutmeg over it.

209

COLD BRANDY FLIP

Use large bar glass

One teaspoon powdered sugar   One fresh egg
One wineglass of brandy   Two lumps of ice
One-half wineglass of water

Dissolve the sugar in the water, add the brandy, egg, and ice, shake up thoroughly, strain into a small bar glass. Serve with a little nutmeg on top.

HOT BRANDY FLIP

Use large bar glass, heated

One teaspoon of sugar   Yolk of one egg
One wineglass of brandy

Dissolve the sugar in a little hot water, add the brandy and egg, shake up thoroughly, pour into a medium bar glass, and fill it one-half full of boiling water. Grate a little nutmeg on top, and serve.

COLD GIN FLIP

Use large bar glass

Same as Cold Rum Flip, substituting Holland gin instead of Jamaica rum.

HOT GIN FLIP

Use large bar glass, heated

Same as Brandy Flip, substituting Holland gin instead of brandy.

213

COLD WHISKEY FLIP

Use large bar glass

Same as Rum Flip, substituting Bourbon or rye whiskey instead of Jamaica rum.

214

HOT WHISKEY FLIP

Same as Brandy Flip, using whiskey instead of brandy.

215

PORT WINE FLIP

Use large bar glass

One small teaspoon of
  powdered white sugar
One large wineglass of
  port wine

One fresh egg
Two or three small lumps
  of ice

Break the egg into the glass, add the sugar, and lastly the wine and ice. Shake up thoroughly and strain into a medium-sized goblet.

SHERRY WINE FLIP

Use large bar glass

This is made precisely as the Port Wine Flip, substituting sherry wine instead or port.

ALE FLIP

Put on the fire in a saucepan one quart of ale, and let it boil; have ready the whites of two eggs and the yolks of four, well beaten up separately; add them by degrees to four tablespoons of moist sugar, and half a nutmeg grated. When all are well mixed, pour on the boiling ale by degrees, beating up the mixture continually; then pour it in rapidly backward and forward from one jug to the other, till the flip is smooth and finely frothed. This is a good remedy to take at the commencement of a cold.

HOT ENGLISH ALE FLIP

One Quart

This is prepared in the same manner as Rum Flip, omitting the rum, and the whites of two of the eggs.

219

EGG FLIP

Put a quart of ale in a saucepan on the fire to boil; in the meantime, beat up the yolks of four, with the whites of two eggs, adding four tablespoons of brown sugar and a little nutmeg; pour on the ale by degrees, beating up, so as to prevent the mixture from curdling; then pour back and forward repeatedly from vessel to vessel, raising the hand to as great a height as possible – which process produces the smoothness and frothing essential to the good quality of the flip. This is excellent for a cold, and from its fleecy appearance, is sometimes designated a 'Yard of Flannel'.

220

EGG FLIP

Another recipe

Beat up, in a jug, four new-laid eggs, omitting two of the whites; add half a dozen large lumps of sugar, and rub these well in the eggs, pour in boiling water, about half a pint at a time, and when the jug is nearly full, throw in two tumblers of Cognac brandy, and one of old Jamaica rum.

FIZZES

GOLDEN FIZ

Use large bar glass

One tablespoon of fine
   white sugar
Three dashes of lemon
   or lime juice

The yolk of one egg
One wineglass of Old Tom gin
Two or three small lumps
   of ice

Shake up thoroughly, strain into a medium bar glass, and fill it up with seltzer water.

SANTA CRUZ FIZ

Use medium bar glass

One teapoon of fine white sugar
Three dashes of lemon juice
One small lump of ice

One wineglass of Santa Cruz
   rum

Fill up the glass with seltzer water from a siphon, or with Apollinaris water, stir thoroughly and serve.

WHISKEY FIZ

Use medium bar glass

One teaspoon of fine white sugar
Three dashes of lemon juice
One small lump of ice

One wineglass of Bourbon or
rye whiskey

Fill the glass up with seltzer or Apollinaris water, stir thoroughly and serve.

BRANDY FIZ

Use medium bar glass

One teaspoon of powdered
white sugar
Three dashes of lemon juice

One wineglass of brandy
One small lump of ice

Fill up the glass with Apollinaris or seltzer water, stir thoroughly and serve.

GIN FIZ

Use medium bar glass

One teaspoon of powdered
  white sugar
Three dashes of lemon juice

One wineglass of Holland gin
One small piece of ice

Fill up the glass with Apollinaris or seltzer water, stir thoroughly and serve.

SILVER FIZ

Use large bar glass

One tablespoon of pulverized
  white sugar
Three dashes of lemon or
  lime juice

The white of one egg
One wineglass of Old Tom gin
Two or three small lumps
  of ice

Shake up thoroughly, strain into a medium bar glass, and fill it up with seltzer water.

SMASHES

This beverage is simply a julep on a small plan.

227

_____

GIN SMASH

Use small bar glass

One-half tablespoon of white sugar	One tablespoon of water One wineglass of gin

Fill two-thirds full of shaved ice; use two sprigs of mint, the same as in the recipe for mint julep. Lay two small pieces of orange on top, and ornament with berries in season.

228

_____

WHISKEY SMASH

Use small bar glass

One-half tablespoon of white sugar	One tablespoon of water One wineglass of whiskey

Fill two-thirds full of shaved ice, and use two sprigs of mint, the same as in the recipe for mint julep.

229

BRANDY SMASH

Use small bar glass

One teaspoon of white sugar
Three or four sprigs of tender
  mint

Two tablespoons of water
One wineglass of brandy

Press the mint in the sugar and water to extract the flavor, add the brandy, and fill the glass two-thirds full of shaved ice. Stir thoroughly, and ornament with a half a slice of orange, and a few fresh sprigs of mint. Serve with a straw. Beautify with berries in season.

SHRUBS

230

CHERRY SHRUB

Pick ripe acid cherries from the stem, and put them in an earthen pot; place that in an iron pot of water; boil till the juice is extracted; strain it through a cloth thick enough to retain the pulp, and sweeten it to your taste. When perfectly clear, bottle it, sealing the cork. By first putting a gill of brandy into each bottle, it will keep throughout the summer. It is delicious mixed with water. Irish or Monongahela whiskey will answer instead of brandy, though not as good.

231

WHITE CURRANT SHRUB

Strip the fruit, and prepare in a jar, as for jelly; strain the juice, of which put two quarts to one gallon of rum, and two pounds of lump sugar; strain through a jelly-bag.

232

CURRANT SHRUB

| One pint of strained currant juice | One pint of sugar |

Boil it gently eight or ten minutes, skimming it well; take it off and, when lukewarm, add half a gill of brandy to every pint of shrub. Bottle tight.

RASPBERRY SHRUB

One quart of vinegar   Three quarts of ripe raspberries

After standing a day, strain it, adding to each pint a pound of sugar, and skim it clear, while boiling about half an hour. Put a wineglass of brandy to each pint of the shrub, when cool. Two spoonfuls of this mixed with a tumbler of water, is an excellent drink in warm weather, and in fevers.

BRANDY SHRUB

To the thin rind of two lemons, and the juice of five, add two quarts of brandy; cover it for three days, then add a quart of sherry and two pounds of loaf sugar, run it through a jelly-bag, and bottle it.

RUM SHRUB

Put three pints of orange juice and one pound of loaf sugar to a gallon of rum. Put all into a cask, and leave it for six weeks, when it will be ready for use.

ENGLISH RUM SHRUB

To three gallons of best Jamaica rum, add a quart of orange juice, a pint of lemon juice, with the peels of the latter fruit cut very thin, and six pounds of the powdered sugar.

Let these be covered close, and remain so all night; next day boil three pints of fresh milk, and let it get cold, then pour it on the spirits and juice, mix them well, and let it stand for an hour. Filter it through a flannel bag lined with blotting paper, into bottles; cork down as soon as each is filled.

COBBLERS

Like the julep, this delicious potation is an American invention, although it is now a favorite in all warm climates. The cobbler does not require much skill in compounding, but to make it acceptable to the eye, as well as to the palate, it is necessary to display some taste in ornamenting the glass after the beverage is made.

237

WHISKEY COBBLER

Use large bar glass

Two wineglasses of whiskey   Two or three slices of orange
One tablespoon of sugar

Fill tumbler with ice, and shake well. Imbibe through a straw.

238

SHERRY COBBLER

Use large bar glass

Two wineglasses of sherry   Two or three slices of orange
One tablespoon of sugar

Fill a tumbler with shaved ice, shake well, and ornament with berries in season. Place a straw in a tasty manner.

CHAMPAGNE COBBLER

One bottle of wine to four large bar glasses

One piece each of orange and   One tablespoon of sugar
    lemon peel

Fill the tumbler one-third full with shaved ice, and fill balance
with wine; ornament in a tasty manner with berries in season.
This beverage should be sipped through a straw.

CATAWBA COBBLER

Use large bar glass

One teaspoon of sugar dissolved   Two wineglasses of wine
    in one tablespoon of water

Fill the tumbler with shaved ice, and ornament with sliced orange
and berries in season. Place a straw as described in the Sherry
Cobbler.

HOCK COBBLER

Use large bar glass

This drink is made the same way as the Catawba Cobbler, using
Hock wine instead of Catawba.

242

CLARET COBBLER

Use large bar glass

This drink is made the same way as the Catawba Cobbler, using claret wine instead of Catawba.

243

SAUTERNE COBBLER

Use large bar glass

The same as Catawba Cobbler, using sauterne instead of Catawba

DAISIES

244

BRANDY DAISY

Use bar glass

Three or four dashes of gum
   syrup
Two or three dashes of curaçao
   cordial

The juice of half a small lemon
One small wineglass of brandy
Two dashes of Jamaica rum

Fill glass one-third full of shaved ice.

   Shake well, strain into a large cocktail glass, and fill up with seltzer water from a siphon.

245

WHISKEY DAISY

Use small bar glass

Three dashes gum syrup
The juice of half a small
   lemon

Two dashes of orgeat syrup
One wineglass of Bourbon,
   or rye whiskey

Fill glass one-third full of shaved ice.

   Shake up thoroughly, strain into a large cocktail glass, and fill up with Apollinaris or seltzer water.

SANTA CRUZ RUM DAISY

Use small bar glass

Three or four dashes of gum
   syrup
Two or three dashes of
   maraschino or curaçao

The juice of half a small
   lemon
One wineglass of Santa Cruz
   rum

Fill glass one-third full of shaved ice.

Shake up thoroughly, strain into a large cocktail glass, and fill up with Apollinaris or seltzer water.

GIN DAISY

Use small bar glass

Three or four dashes of orgeat,
   or gum syrup
Three dashes of maraschino

The juice of half a small lemon
One wineglass of Holland gin

Fill glass one-third full of shaved ice.

Shake up thoroughly, strain into a large cocktail glass, and fill up with Apollinaris or seltzer water.

TOM COLLINS

248

TOM COLLINS WHISKEY

Use small bar glass

Five or six dashes of gum syrup   One large wineglass of whiskey
Juice of a small lemon   Two or three lumps of ice

Shake well and strain into a large bar glass.
    Fill up the glass with plain soda water and imbibe while it is lively.

249

TOM COLLINS GIN

Use large bar glass

The same as Tom Collins Whiskey, substituting gin for whiskey.

250

TOM COLLINS BRANDY

Use large bar glass

The same as Tom Collins Whiskey, substituting brandy for whiskey.

FIXES

In making fixes be careful and put the lemon skin in the glass.

WHISKEY FIX

One large teaspoon of powdered white sugar, dissolved in a little water

The juice of half a lemon
One wineglass of Bourbon or rye whiskey

Fill up the glass about two-thirds full of shaved ice, stir well, and ornament the top of the glass.

BRANDY FIX

Use small bar glass

One tablespoon of sugar
One-fourth of a lemon

One-half a wineglass of water
One wineglass of brandy

Fill a tumbler two-thirds full of shaved ice. Stir with a spoon, and dress the top with fruit in season.

GIN FIX

Use small bar glass

One tablespoon of sugar
One-fourth of a lemon

One-half a wineglass of water
One wineglass of gin

Fill two-thirds full of shaved ice. Stir with a spoon, and ornament the top with fruits in season.

SANTA CRUZ FIX

The Santa Cruz fix is made by substituting Santa Cruz rum instead of brandy.

SOURS

In making sours be careful and put the lemon skin in the glass.

255

GIN SOUR

Use small bar glass

The gin sour is made with the same ingredients as the gin fix, omitting all fruits, except a small piece of lemon, the juice of which must be pressed in the glass.

256

SANTA CRUZ SOUR

The Santa Cruz sour is made by substituting Santa Cruz rum instead of gin.

BRANDY SOUR

Use small bar glass

One teaspoon of powdered white sugar, dissolved in a little Apollinaris or seltzer water

The juice of half a lemon
One wineglass of brandy
One dash of curaçao

Fill the glass with shaved ice, shake, and strain into a claret glass.

EGG SOUR

Use small bar glass

One teaspoon of powdered white sugar
Three dashes of lemon juice
One pony of curaçao

One pony of brandy
One egg
Two or three small lumps of ice

Shake up well, and remove the ice before serving.

TODDIES

259

APPLE TODDY

Use small bar glass

One tablespoon of fine
white sugar

One wineglass of cider brandy
One-half of a baked apple

Fill the glass two-thirds full of boiling water, and grate a little nutmeg on top.

260

BRANDY TODDY

Use small bar glass

One teaspoon of sugar
One-half wineglass of water

One wineglass of brandy
One small lump of ice

Stir with a spoon.

HOT BRANDY TODDY

Use small bar glass, hot

One teaspoon of fine white sugar

One wineglass of brandy

Dissolve the sugar in a little boiling water, add the brandy, and pour boiling water into the glass until it is two-thirds full. Grate a little nutmeg on top.

WHISKEY TODDY

Use small bar glass

One teaspoon of sugar
One-half wineglass of water

One wineglass of whiskey
One small lump of ice

Stir with a spoon.

GIN TODDY

One teaspoon of sugar
One-half wineglass of water

One wineglass of gin
One small lump of ice

Stir with a spoon.

264

HOT GIN TODDY

Use small bar glass, hot

One teaspoon of powdered white sugar	One wineglass of Holland, or Old Tom gin (as preferred)

Dissolve the sugar in boiling water, add the gin, and pour boiling water into the glass until it is two-thirds full.

SLINGS

265

BRANDY SLING

Use small bar glass

One small teaspoon of
  powdered white sugar
One wineglass of water

One small lump of ice
One small wineglass of brandy

Dissolve the sugar in water, add the brandy and ice, stir well with a spoon. Grate a little nutmeg on top, and serve.

266

HOT BRANDY SLING

Use medium bar glass, hot

One small teaspoon
  of powdered sugar

One wineglass of brandy

Dissolve the sugar in a little boiling water, add the brandy, and fill the glass two-thirds full of boiling water. Grate a little nutmeg on top and serve.

HOT WHISKEY SLING

Use small bar glass

One wineglass of whiskey

Fill tumbler one-third full with boiling water, and grate nutmeg on top.

GIN SLING

Use small bar glass

The gin sling is made with the same ingredients as the gin toddy, except you grate a little nutmeg on top.

WHISKEY SLING

Use small bar glass

One small tablespoon of powdered white sugar
One wineglass of water

One wineglass of Bourbon or rye whiskey

Dissolve the sugar in the water, add the whiskey and ice, stir thoroughly with a spoon. Grate a little nutmeg on top, and serve.

SANGAREES

270

PORT WINE SANGAREE

Use small bar glass

One and one-third wineglass   One teaspoon of sugar
   of port wine

Fill tumbler two-thirds with ice. Shake well and grate nutmeg on top.

271

SHERRY SANGAREE

Use small bar glass

One wineglass of sherry   One teaspoon of fine sugar

Fill tumbler one-third with ice, and grate nutmeg on top.

272

BRANDY SANGAREE

Use small bar glass

The brandy sangaree is made with the same ingredients as the brandy toddy, adding nutmeg. Fill two-thirds full of ice, and dash about a teaspoon of port wine, so that it will float on top.

GIN SANGAREE

Use small bar glass

The gin sangaree is made with the same ingredients as the gin toddy, adding nutmeg. Fill two-thirds with ice, and dash about a teaspoon of port wine, so that it will float on the top.

ALE SANGAREE.

Use large bar glass

One teaspoon of sugar, dissolved in a tablespoon of water.

Fill the tumbler with ale, and grate nutmeg on top.

PORTER SANGAREE

Use large bar glass

This beverage is made the same as an ale sangaree, and is sometimes called portaree.

SKINS

276

SCOTCH WHISKY SKIN

Use small bar glass

One wineglass of Scotch
  whisky

One piece of lemon peel

Fill the tumbler one-half full of boiling water.

277

IRISH WHISKEY SKIN

Use small bar glass

One lump of white sugar
One wineglass of Irish
  whiskey

One small piece of lemon
  peel

Proceed as directed for Scotch Whisky Skin.

278

COLUMBIA SKIN

This is a Boston drink, and is made the same as a Whiskey Skin.

SYRUPS, ESSENCES, TINCTURES, COLORINGS, ETC.

279

SOLFERINO COLORING

One gallon of alcohol (95 percent)

One ounce of solferino

Put them in a bottle, shake well, and in twenty-four hours it will be ready for use.

280

CARAMEL

Seven pounds of loaf sugar

One pint of water

Crush and dissolve the sugar in the water; boil it in a five-gallon copper kettle, stirring occasionally, until it gets brown; when it begins to burn, reduce the fire; let it burn until the smoke becomes offensive to the eyes; then try it by dipping a rod into it, and letting a few drops fall into a glass of cold water; if it settles at the bottom and crystallizes, so that it will crack, it is done. Then take about half a gallon of lukewarm water, and pour it in by degrees, stirring all the time. When thoroughly mixed, filter it while hot through a coarse flannel filter.

ESSENCE OF COGNAC

One ounce of oil of cognac
One-half gallon of spirits
(95 percent)
One gallon of spirits
(70 percent)

Two ounces of strong
ammonia
One pound of fine black tea
Two pounds of prunes

Dissolve the oil of cognac in the 95 percent spirits; cork it tightly in a bottle and let it stand for three days, frequently shaking it, then add the ammonia.

Mash the prunes (breaking the kernels) and put them with the tea and the 70 percent spirits into a stone jar of three gallons capacity; cover closely, and let it stand for eight days.

Filter the liquor, and add it to the solution of oil and ammonia. Bottle for use.

This quantity is sufficient for flavoring 100 gallons of brandy.

ESSENCE OF LEMON

One ounce of oil of lemon
One quart of alcohol
(95 percent)

One-half pint of water
One and one-half ounces
of citric acid

Grind the citric acid to a powder in a porcelain mortar; dissolve it in the water. Then cut the oil of lemon in the alcohol, and add the acid water.

LEMON SYRUP

Five gallons of gum syrup   One ounce of oil of lemon
Four ounces of tartaric acid   One pint of alcohol

Cut the oil of lemon in the alcohol, add the tartaric acid, and mix thoroughly with the syrup.

GUM SYRUP

Fourteen pounds of loaf sugar   One gallon of water

Boil together for five minutes, and add water to make up to two gallons.

AROMATIC TINCTURE

One ounce of ginger   One-half ounce of valerian
One ounce of cinnamon   Two quarts of alcohol
One ounce of orange peel

Macerate the ingredients in the alcohol in a close vessel for fourteen days, then filter through filtering paper. This is sometimes employed to give a flavor to milk punch, but it must be used with precaution. Ten drops are sufficient for a pint of punch.

286

TINCTURE OF CINNAMON.

Place two pounds of ground cinnamon in a jar with one gallon 95 percent alcohol, closely covered. At the end of eight days strain the liquor clear; wash the sediment with one quart proof spirits; strain it; mix the two liquors together, and filter through blotting paper.

287

TINCTURE OF CLOVES

Take one pound of ground cloves; warm them over a fire until quite hot; put them quickly into a jar, pour on them one gallon 95 percent alcohol, cover them airtight, and let them stand for ten days. Draw off into bottles and cork close.

288

TINCTURE OF ORANGE PEEL

One pound of dried orange peel (ground)	One gallon of spirits (95 percent)

Place them in a closely corked vessel for ten days. Strain and bottle for use.

289

TINCTURE OF LEMON PEEL

Cut into small chips the peel of twelve large lemons. Place it in a glass jar and pour over it one gallon spirits, 70 percent. Let it stand until the lemon peel has all sunk to the bottom of the liquor. It is then ready for use without either filtering or straining.

290

TINCTURE OF ALL-SPICE

This is prepared in the same manner as tincture of cinnamon, using ground all-spice instead of cinnamon.

TEMPERANCE DRINKS

291

MILK AND SELTZER

Use large soda glass

Fill the glass half full of milk, and the remaining half with seltzer water.

292

LEMONADE POWDERS

One pound of finely powdered loaf sugar, one ounce of tartaric or citric acid, and twenty drops of essence of lemon. Mix, and keep very dry. Two or three teaspoons of this stirred briskly in a tumbler of water will make a very pleasant glass of lemonade. If effervescent lemonade be desired, one ounce of carbonate of soda must be added to the above.

LEMONADE

Use large bar glass

The rind of two lemons
Juice of three large lemons

One-half pound of loaf sugar
One quart of boiling water

Rub some of the sugar, in lumps, on two of the lemons until they have imbibed all the oil from them, and put it with the remainder of the sugar into a jug; add the lemon juice (but no pits) and pour over the whole a quart of boiling water. When the sugar has dissolved, strain the lemonade through a piece of muslin, and, when cool, it will be ready for use.

The lemonade will be much improved by having the white of an egg beaten up with it; a little sherry mixed with it also makes this beverage much nicer.

ORANGEADE

This agreeable beverage is made the same way as lemonade, substituting oranges for lemons.

ORGEAT LEMONADE

Use large bar glass

One-half wineglass of   The juice of half a lemon
  orgeat syrup

Fill the tumbler one-third full of ice, and balance with water.
Shake well, and ornament with berries in season.

GINGER LEMONADE

Boil twenty pounds and a half of lump sugar for twenty minutes in
ten gallons of water; clear it with the whites of six eggs. Bruise half
a pound of common ginger, boil with the liquor, and then pour
it upon ten lemons pared. When quite cold, put it in a cask, with
two tablespoons of yeast, the lemons sliced, and half an ounce
of isinglass. Bung up the cask the next day; it will be ready in two
weeks.

SODA LEMONADE

Use large soda glass

One and one-half tablespoons
of powdered white sugar

Juice of half a lemon

One bottle of plain soda water

Two or three small lumps
of ice

Stir up well, and remove the ice before serving.

Seltzer Lemonade may be made by substituting seltzer water for the soda.

EGG LEMONADE

Use large bar glass

One large tablespoon of
pulverized white sugar.

Juice of half a lemon

One fresh egg

Two or three small lumps
of ice

Shake up thoroughly, strain into a soda-water glass and fill up the glass with soda or seltzer water. Ornament with berries.

SODA NECTAR

Use large tumbler

Juice of one lemon

Three-quarters tumblerful
of water

Powdered white sugar to taste

One-half small teaspoon
of carbonate of soda

Strain the juice of the lemon, and add it to the water, with sufficient white sugar to sweeten the whole nicely. When well mixed, put in the soda, stir well, and drink while the mixture is in an effervescing state.

DRINK FOR THE DOG DAYS

A bottle of soda water poured into a large goblet, in which a lemon ice has been placed, forms a deliciously cool and refreshing drink; but should be taken with some care, and positively avoided whilst you are very hot.

SHERBET

Eight ounces of carbonate of soda, six ounces of tartaric acid, two pounds of loaf sugar (finely powdered), three drachms of essence of lemon. Let the powders be *very dry*. Mix them intimately, and keep them for use in a wide-mouthed bottle, closely corked. Put two good-sized teaspoons into a tumbler; pour in half a pint of cold water, stir briskly, and drink off.

LEMON SHERBET

Four lemons sliced, four ounces of lump sugar, one quart of boiling water. Very fine. A cheaper drink may be made thus: one ounce of cream of tartar, one ounce tartaric or citric acid, the juice and peel of two lemons, and half a pound, or more, of loaf sugar. The sweetening must be regulated according to taste.

IMPERIAL DRINK FOR FAMILIES

Two ounces of cream of tartar, the juice and peel of two or three lemons, and half a pound of coarse sugar. Put these into a gallon pitcher, and pour on boiling water. When cool it will be fit for use.

NECTAR

One drachm of citric acid, one scruple of bicarbonate of potash, one ounce of white sugar, powdered. Fill a soda-water bottle nearly full of water, drop in the potash and sugar, and lastly the citric acid. Cork the bottle up *immediately*, and shake. As soon as the crystals are dissolved, the nectar is fit for use. It may be colored with a small portion of cochineal.

RASPBERRY, STRAWBERRY, CURRANT OR ORANGE EFFERVESCING DRAUGHTS

Take one quart of the juice of either of the above fruits, filter it, and boil it into a syrup, with one pound of powdered loaf sugar. To this add one ounce and a half of tartaric acid. When cold put it into a bottle, and keep it well corked. When required for use, fill a half-pint tumbler three parts full of water, and add two tablespoons of the syrup. Then stir in briskly a small teaspoon of carbonate of soda, and a very delicious drink will be formed. The color may be improved by adding a very small portion of cochineal to the syrup at the time of boiling.

GINGER WINE

Put twelve pounds of loaf sugar and six ounces of powdered ginger into six gallons of water; let it boil for an hour, then beat up the whites of half a dozen eggs with a whisk, and mix them well with the liquor. When quite cold put it into a barrel, with six lemons cut into slices, and a cupful of yeast; let it work for three days, then put in the bung. In a week's time you may bottle it, and it will be ready for immediate use.

NOTES

1. With a grain of salt.
2. Alexis Benoît Soyer (1810–58), French by birth, was arguably the most famous chef in nineteenth-century London.
3. Colonel T.B. Thorpe was an American author and a Republican politician.
4. Roswell Hart (1824–83) was a Republican politician from New York.
5. Henry William Herbert (1807–58) was an English novelist, translator and writer on sport, and a man of notoriously dissolute habits.
6. Charles Godfrey Leland (1824–1903) was an American author and humorist.
7. Gulian Crommelin Verplanck (1786–1870) was a notable New York politician.
8. Bayard Taylor (1825–78) was an American poet, author and critic.
9. Jerry Thomas advises the use of bar glasses in making cocktails as the modern cocktail shaker had not yet been invented.
10. Now called Martini.
11. Thomas Dunn English (1819–1902) was an American politician, author and songwriter.
12. From Badminton House, Gloucestershire, the seat of the Duke of Beaufort.
13. The Blue Blazer was Jerry Thomas' signature drink, famous for the spectacular method of preparation.
14. This was the personal recipe of William Henry Harrison, the ninth president of the United States.
15. Colonel Francis Negus, of the English Army, who died in 1732.
16. Charles Dibdin (1745–1814) was an English writer and musician.

GLOSSARY

All-spice: the dried unripe fruit of the *Pimenta dioica* plant, very popular in Caribbean cooking

Ambergris: a highly prized substance; a bilious secretion from the intestines of sperm whales, primarily used as a fixative in perfumes

Applejack: concentrated cider created by distillation or freeze distillation

Arrack: an alcoholic drink made largely in South and South-East Asia by fermenting fruit, rice, molasses or palm sap

Bloom raisins: one of three kinds of raisins produced from Spanish or Malaga raisins and characterized by the bluish tint of the grape

Capillaire: originally a syrup prepared from *Adiantum capillus Veneris*, or maidenhair fern, and flavored with orange flower water. Eventually, it came to refer to any syrup made with orange flowers or orange essence. See recipes Nos. 65–6

Catawba: a purple-red grape grown principally on the east coast of the United States, and the wine deriving from this grape

Demijohn: a large bottle with a short, narrow neck, which holds up to 10 gallons of water. Usually encased in wicker

Drachm: also spelt 'dram', ⅛ fl oz or 3.5 ml

Gentian: flower growing in mountainous regions, the root of which can be used in the preparation of alcoholic drinks

Gill: approximately 5 fl oz or 142 ml

Gum syrup: syrup made from water and sugar solution, using the edible gum of an acacia tree as an emulsifier

Hockheimer: a wine produced at Hochheim, near Mainz in Germany

Isabella: a wine made from the Isabella grape, which is found mainly on the east coast of the United States, in South America, and in Eastern Europe

Isinglass: a type of collagen taken from the gas bladders of fish, widely used before the cheap production of gelatine

Kirschwasser: German for 'cherry water'; a clear, colourless fruit brandy made by distilling whole cherries

Kumyss: also spelt 'kumis'; a dairy product made using mare's milk, fermented in order to give it alcoholic properties. Popular in Turkey and other Middle Eastern countries

Moselle: a German white wine from the valley of the river Moselle, near the French border

Noyau: Crème de Noyau, a cordial of brandy flavored with the kernel of a bitter almond or a peach stone

Orgeat syrup: made using almonds, sugar and rosewater; a sweet syrup with a distinct almond taste

Pony: approximately 1 fl oz or 28 ml

Porter: a dark beer, related to but less potent than stout

Potash (or potash water): a sparkling water produced using an impure form of potassium carbonate. Generally no longer used in the production of drinks

Quart: approximately 32 fl oz or 910 ml

Rock candy: confectionery made up of large sugar crystals of refined pure cane sugar

Scruple: approximately ½4 fl oz

Sauterne: a sweet wine deriving from the Sauternes region of Bordeaux, France

Shrub: an old English alcoholic cordial emanating from the West Country, typically used to complement rum

Solferino: a magenta dye. See recipe No. 279

Tincture: alcoholic extract of plant material with an ethanol percentage of at least 40–60. See recipes Nos. 285–90

Verbena: family of mainly tropical plants of which lemon verbena is now the most commonly used

Wormwood: *Artemisia absinthum*, a plant commonly known as an ingredient of absinthe and used to flavor vermouth. Pure oil of wormwood is very dangerous; it can cause kidney failure and death and is present in authentic absinthe only in very small quantities

BIOGRAPHICAL NOTE

Jerry Thomas (1830–85), often nicknamed 'Professor' Jerry Thomas, is seen as 'the father of American mixology'. Born in Jefferson County, New York, he trained as a bartender in Connecticut before moving to California. Although he returned to New York in 1851 and ultimately settled there, the early years of his career saw him travelling and working throughout the United States and in Europe. He excelled in the performance elements of mixology, becoming renowned for his elaborate techniques and flashy style.

Thomas published the first edition of *How to Mix Drinks* in 1862, and in so doing invented the cocktail book and the formal cocktail recipe, which had previously been passed on only orally. He would come to revise and augment the book several times in the course of his lifetime, notably giving greater prominence to cocktail recipes, which formed only a small part of the initial publication.

The posts for which he was most famous were as head bartender at New York's Metropolitan Hotel, and at his own bar on Broadway in New York. He was a recognised man about town, although while in New York he married and had two daughters. He lost his fortune in ill-advised speculation on Wall Street and was forced to sell his bar. This was a blow both professionally and personally, and his subsequent ventures never achieved the success that he had enjoyed earlier in life. He died of apoplexy in New York in 1885, at the age of fifty-five.